A LifeGuide®

M000031650

SERVICE

Ministry with Heart and Hands

10 STUDIES FOR INDIVIDUALS OR GROUPS

R. Paul Stevens

With Notes for Leaders

IVP Connect

An imprint of InterVarsity Press
Downers Grove, Illinois

InterVarsity Press
P.O. Box 1400, Downers Grove, IL 60515-1426
World Wide Web: www.ivpress.com
Email: email@ivpress.com

*InterVarsity Press® is the book-publishing division of InterVarsity Christian Fellowship/USA®, a
movement of students and faculty active on campus at hundreds of universities, colleges and schools
of nursing in the United States of America, and a member movement of the International Fellowship
of Evangelical Students. For information about local and regional activities, write Public Relations
Dept., InterVarsity Christian Fellowship/USA, 6400 Schroeder Rd., P.O. Box 7895, Madison, WI
53707-7895, or visit the IVCF website at www.intervarsity.org.*

*While all stories in this book are true, some names and identifying information in this book have
been changed to protect the privacy of the individuals involved.*

Cover design: Beth McGill
Cover image: ©arlindo71/iStockphoto

ISBN 978-0-8308-3106-7 (print)
ISBN 978-0-8308-6399-0 (digital)

Printed in the United States of America ♾

P	18	17	16	15	14	13	12	11	10	9	8	7	6	5	4	3	2	1
Y	31	30	29	28	27	26	25	24	23	22	21	20	19	18	17	16	15

Contents

Getting the Most Out of *Service*

One of the great things about the Christian way is that it eliminates the divide between the sacred and the secular, especially in the area of service. In most religious systems those who preach, baptize and lead worship are doing sacred service, while people who make meals or deals are doing secular work. This false divide was smashed by Jesus. The good news Jesus preached and embodied is that all of life and all service to others can be part of the kingdom of God—that glorious shalom-bringing rule of God that infects life in this world with heaven.

Usually when we speak of service we refer to something done for the benefit of others. But in both languages of the Bible, Greek and Hebrew, *ministry* and *service* are the same word. So in this series of studies we are considering biblical examples of people doing ministry. But here is the problem. Sometimes ministry is defined by (1) *place*—service *in* the church building rather than the marketplace and home, (2) *function*—something done on behalf of the whole, such as pastoral ministration, (3) *need*—meeting "spiritual" needs rather than secular needs such as servicing an automobile, and (4) *title*—such as Reverend. But in the New Testament ministry is something that belongs to all of God's people, all men and women, all old and young, and it is not just done in churches and mission fields but in workplaces, cities, relationships, schools and universities, hospitals and medical clinics, and art studios. No wonder good Christian people are confused.

Many of us have been told that some people do ministry more than others, that not everything is ministry, that ministry may relate to certain functions more than others but may "happen" in almost any context, that ministry is done by some full time and by others part time, and that ministry par excellence is what the pastor does. And no wonder the confusion when good pastors hear of someone's call into ministry, they think instinctively of preaching and other ministry functions. If ministry is evangelizing the lost and edifying the found, then only a small minority of the church can do ministry continuously, perhaps the one percent that can be supported financially for so-called full-time ministry. In reality there are no part-time options available. For the rest of the people of God, ministry is a discretionary time activity—something done with the few hours that can be squeezed out of the week's schedule after working, sleeping, parenting, neighboring, washing and doing the chores.

The Bible addresses this massive confusion with a liberating perspective: ministry is *service to God and neighbor at the same time*. Ministers are people who put themselves at the disposal of God for the benefit of others and God's world. It is not limited by the place where the service is rendered, the function, the need met by the title of the person or even by an overt reference to Christ. In Matthew 25:31-46 the surprise of the righteous on the day of judgment is that the service done gratuitously for others was actually done for Christ, and the concern of the unrighteous was just this: if they had known it was Jesus they were serving, they would gladly have done it. So service and ministry are totally interchangeable ways of speaking of the same reality. It might be a good thing if we could permanently substitute the word *service* wherever we now use the word *ministry*. Imagine someone saying, "I have been called into service in the church." Or I am called into ministry in the school, the hospital or the company.

In the following ten studies, covering examples from Genesis to Revelation, we will explore service in a variety of contexts: family, the physical creation, society, the city, neighbors, relationships, the church and the workplace. Looking inside ministry we will examine examples of service that were motivated by imagination, passion, faith, hope and love. Out of these studies I hope you will discover that you are a full-time minister of Jesus Christ and be able to live and serve wholeheartedly.

Suggestions for Individual Study

1. As you begin each study, pray that God will speak to you through his Word.

2. Read the introduction to the study and respond to the personal reflection question or exercise. This is designed to help you focus on God and on the theme of the study.

3. Each study deals with a particular passage so that you can delve into the author's meaning in that context. Read and reread the passage to be studied. The questions are written using the language of the New International Version, so you may wish to use that version of the Bible. The New Revised Standard Version is also recommended.

4. This is an inductive Bible study, designed to help you discover for yourself what Scripture is saying. The study includes three types of questions. Observation questions ask about the basic facts: who, what, when, where and how. Interpretation questions delve into the meaning of the passage. Application questions help you discover the implications of the text for growing in Christ. These three keys unlock the treasures of Scripture.

Write your answers to the questions in the spaces provided or in a personal journal. Writing can bring clarity and deeper understanding of yourself and of God's Word.

5. It might be good to have a Bible dictionary handy. Use it to look up any unfamiliar words, names or places.

6. Use the prayer suggestion to guide you in thanking God for what you have learned and to pray about the applications that have come to mind.

7. You may want to go on to the suggestion under "Now or Later," or you may want to use that idea for your next study.

Suggestions for Members of a Group Study

1. Come to the study prepared. Follow the suggestions for individual study mentioned above. You will find that careful preparation will greatly enrich your time spent in group discussion.

2. Be willing to participate in the discussion. The leader of your group will not be lecturing. Instead, he or she will be encouraging the members of the group to discuss what they have learned. The leader will be asking the questions that are found in this guide.

3. Stick to the topic being discussed. Your answers should be based on the verses which are the focus of the discussion and not on outside authorities such as commentaries or speakers. These studies focus on a particular passage of Scripture. Only rarely should you refer to other portions of the Bible. This allows for everyone to participate in in-depth study on equal ground.

4. Be sensitive to the other members of the group. Listen attentively when they describe what they have learned. You may be surprised by their insights! Each question assumes a variety of answers. Many questions do not have "right" answers, particularly questions that aim at meaning or application. Instead the questions push us to explore the passage more thoroughly.

When possible, link what you say to the comments of others. Also, be affirming whenever you can. This will encourage some of the more hesitant members of the group to participate.

5. Be careful not to dominate the discussion. We are sometimes so eager to express our thoughts that we leave too little opportunity for others to respond. By all means participate! But allow others to also.

6. Expect God to teach you through the passage being discussed and through the other members of the group. Pray that you will have an enjoyable and profitable time together, but also that as a result of the study you will find ways that you can take action individually and/or as a group.

7. Remember that anything said in the group is considered confidential and should not be discussed outside the group unless specific permission is given to do so.

8. If you are the group leader, you will find additional suggestions at the back of the guide.

1

Caring for Creation

Adam and Eve

The Bible opens with an amazing picture of God serving, God working. Unlike the gods of the Greco-Roman mythologies, God is not dining on nectar and ambrosia in heavenly rest and contemplation. God is busy fashioning everything and giving meaning to it. In a story that could be understood by the simplest Bedouin nomad or the most sophisticated nuclear scientist, a figurative account of a literal event, the fundamental truth about God, humankind and the world is expressed. Galileo Galilei once said, "The Bible tells us how to go to heaven, not how the heavens go." It tells us who created and why, and science continues to tell us how.

GROUP DISCUSSION. Think of a situation in which you were involved in what seemed a completely meaningless activity. What made it seem that way, and how could it have been different?

PERSONAL REFLECTION. Have you ever been given a job description? If so, how did it make you feel? What difference did it make to how you functioned?

The earlier part of Genesis 1 describes God speaking everything into creation—first by separating and then by filling everything, creating place. God made everything nonhuman and then, as his superlative creation, he made a creature that is absolutely distinct. In so making human beings in two sexes and commissioning us, God gave us both our identity and our calling (our being and our doing). *Read Genesis 1:1–2:15.*

---

1. Describe what we learn about God in the first chapter of Genesis.

What do we learn about the world and universe we live in?

In contrast what would it be like to live in a universe that was all chaos rather than a cosmos?

---

2. Genesis 1:26 states that God made human beings in his image and likeness. From what you read in Genesis 1–2 what are the characteristics that make us reflect God?

---

3. By placing human beings in a garden where God is present (Genesis 3:8), in a social community and in an undeveloped material world, what do you think the job description is for the humans?

4. What is your own response to this description of what it means to be a person serving God and God's purposes?

5. Since the words *serve* and *ministry* are the same in both original languages of Scripture, how would you describe in your own words the ministry of all human beings?

6. The first instance of the word *holy* in the Bible is found in Genesis 2:3. What is so good about the rest commandment God places on human work?

7. Genesis 2 restates the story of creation from a different perspective, as though to answer the question, How does it take both man and woman to be in the image of God? What further perspective do you gain from this chapter on the dignity and the duty of human beings?

How do you see this being fulfilled in your own life and service?

8. The various terms used for Adam and Eve's service description include "be fruitful," "increase in number," "fill the earth," "rule," "work [the earth]" and "take care of it" (see Genesis 1:28; 2:15). Describe how these are fulfilled in the various ordinary occupations, whether paid or not, that we undertake today.

---

9. What difference will viewing everyday tasks as service and ministry to God and neighbor make to how you live and work in the world?

Thank God for showing you the rich and fruitful service that he calls all human beings to undertake. Ask him to help you see how your own work serves him, your neighbor and his creation.

Now or Later

Read the rest of the creation story in Genesis 2:16–3:19. What has happened to the man and woman, to the creation? What affect has sin on everyday work and service, and on the relationship of husband and wife? Why has this come about? What indicates that the man and woman have not lost everything that constitutes their uniqueness as God's image-bearing creatures? Does God want us to live this way now, and if not, why?

2

Witnessing
About Jesus

The Samaritan Woman

John 4:1-42

"You Christians are so bigoted! You think that you have the only way to God." This outburst happened after several weeks in a neighborhood Bible study with atheists and adherents of an Eastern religion. It cut deeply. I responded carefully, "Yes you are right. We Christians are often bigoted. But Jesus is not. He includes everyone." The study we are undertaking in the fourth Gospel of the New Testament is an extraordinary example of the inclusiveness of Jesus, and the natural witnessing that comes from being truly and deeply welcomed by him. At the time of Jesus the old divided kingdom of Judah (in the south) and Israel-Samaria (in the north) suffered deep animosities toward each other. The Samaritans, remnants of the old kingdom that got shifted off to Assyria, with their own temple on Mount Gerizim, and with a small Bible composed only of the first five books as God's Word, were loathed by most Jews, especially the strict Pharisees. If at all possible they avoided even passing through their territory. They were "unclean." But Jesus deliberately goes there, meets a woman by Jacob's well and initiates an amazing conversation. It becomes a model for witnessing. Significantly this conversation takes place in the woman's workplace. It is generally agreed that in the twenty-first century the primary location for the mission of God is the marketplace, not the church or religious gatherings.

GROUP DISCUSSION. In the North and West of the world, and in some other regions in Asia and the Middle East, political correctness often dictates that references to Jesus and the Christian faith are not allowed in public schools, political arenas and workplaces. But questions are often raised about life issues, death and the afterlife, and hungers of the heart for forgiveness and reconciliation. Give some examples of situations members of your group have encountered that were invitations to share their own convictions.

PERSONAL REFLECTION. Think of the last time you enthusiastically shared a discovery (not necessarily spiritual) you had made. What motivated you? Was the occasion planned or did it just "happen?" How was it received?

In the first study we considered how, in God's plan for his God-imaging creature, we would serve God, neighbor and the world through building community and developing the potential of creation—pro-creativity and co-creativity. In this study we consider the service/ministry which belongs not just to human beings in general but to *all* followers of Jesus, not just clergy and missionaries. *Read John 4:1-42.*

1. Trace the development of Jesus' conversation with the woman.

- What does he say?

- What does she hear?

- How does he respond to her misunderstanding?

- How does he probe deeper?

2. What do we learn about Jesus from his actions when he meets the Samaritan woman?

3. Why do you think Jesus asked for help in getting water?

Why was the woman so surprised?

---

4. When do you think it is appropriate to ask someone you wish to introduce to Jesus to help and serve you?

Can you give any examples of ways that not-yet-Christians have served and ministered to you?

---

5. Why do you think Jesus confronted the woman with her life of sin (vv. 16-18)?

---

6. The woman either tries a diversionary tactic to get Jesus off the subject of her live-in lover or perhaps she is genuinely concerned about what would be the right place to offer a sacrifice for her sin. How does Jesus turn this shift in the conversation into a challenge and the offering of good news?

---

7. Trace the development of the woman's recognition of Jesus through all its stages from "a man" to finally, with the townspeople, "the Savior of the world."

8. What do the disciples learn about Jesus and the kingdom of God when they return with food (vv. 27-38)?

---

9. What is so constructive about the way the Samaritan woman witnessed to her townspeople about Jesus (vv. 28-29)?

---

10. What have you learned from this story about witnessing about Jesus when, as is the case in much of the world today, there is no expectation of a Messiah or a Savior of the world?

Ask our gracious God to open your eyes and ears to hear when there are openings to share the gospel and grant wisdom in listening and speaking.

Now or Later

In a society where women were second class and subjugated, Jesus consistently treated women as equals with men and with dignity. The Samaritan woman is a case in point. This is the first and the only occasion where Jesus admits he is the Messiah before his trial, and this to a woman. Though the core twelve disciples were men, Jesus included women in the traveling discipleship community, and they supplied his needs from their own funds (Luke 8:3). Jesus never spoke disparagingly of women or suggested that they were subordinate to men or their husbands. Women were the last at the cross and the first at the tomb. The Lord trusted his first evangelistic witness after his resurrection to a woman (John 20:18).

Write down instances of where women in your own context—church, college group or social setting—have rendered significant service. Also write down situations where women in our own context have been treated as second class in service. What do you think can be done about it?

3

Building Up the People of God

Priscilla and Aquila

There is nothing in the world like the church. And nothing like the every-member ministry that is the constitutional framework of the New Testament people of God. Sometimes it is called "a holy priesthood" or a "royal priesthood" (1 Peter 2:5, 9), which means that everyone in Christ has direct access to God (without the need of a human intermediary), everyone is a priest to other believers—touching them for God—and the believing community is a priest to the world, bringing the presence and purpose of God. When people are joined to Christ they immediately are joined to the body of Christ, the people of God. There are no individual believers, no unchurched Christians. So when Christians gather, they are not consumers getting "spine-tingling" worship or professional sermons. They gather for mutual edification.

GROUP DISCUSSION. Discuss the following conversation from George MacDonald's novel *The Curate's Awakening*.

> "The great evil in the church has always been the presence in it of persons unsuited for the work required of them there. One

very simple sifting rule would be, that no one should be admitted to the clergy who had not first proved himself capable of making a better living in some other calling." . . . "I was thinking," responded Polwarth, "mainly of the experience in life he would gather by having to make his own living. Behind the counter or the plough, or in the workshop, he would come to know men and their struggles and their thoughts."*

PERSONAL REFLECTION. Recall an experience of "being ministered to." Who was the person? What did the person do? How did he or she do it? What effect did it have?

In this study we turn to Acts, usually called the "Acts of the Apostles," but really, as Dr. Luke, the author, indicates in Acts 1:1, it records the things Jesus "began to do and to teach" through the apostles and all the believers after Jesus ascended to heaven. Much of the book contains the apostle Paul's travel and ministry experiences as he pushed the frontiers of the kingdom of God beyond the Jewish world. In the passage we are studying Paul was traveling from Corinth with a couple, Priscilla and Aquila, Paul left in Ephesus. They had a significant ministry as tentmakers. Tentmaking means they were self-supporting ministers, in this case by actually sewing goat hair into mobile homes. They are models of every-member ministry and how every believer can serve and equip other believers. *Read Acts 18:18-28.*

---

1. Find a map of Paul's travels (often in a study Bible) and trace the journey of Paul, Priscilla and Aquila from Corinth to Ephesus, and then Paul's continuing journey to Jerusalem and back to Asia Minor (modern-day Turkey) to encourage the new churches. What does Paul do both to himself and for others to facilitate his service to both Jews and Gentiles?

Most likely how did Paul go about "strengthening all the disciples?" (v. 23).

---

2. Among Paul's traveling companions was a couple, Priscilla and Aquila, refugees fleeing from Rome, whom Paul met in Corinth, stayed with and worked alongside in Corinth (Acts 18:1-3). Paul and this couple had the same trade—making goat-hair tents, which they would sell in the marketplace. From other Scriptures we learn that Paul occasionally received financial support from churches, though not directly from churches he was currently serving. But Aquila and Priscilla always supported themselves. What are the advantages of this?

The disadvantages?

---

3. How do you view your own life of work and ministry—integrated as one or separated into sacred and secular? Why?

---

4. From later Scriptures we learn that Aquila and Priscilla were themselves on the move, first Rome, then Corinth, then Ephesus and finally Rome again, where they hosted a church "in their home." What advantages did their trade afford in facilitating their service to others and to churches?

5. What ministries or services would be involved in hosting a church in one's home?

---

6. What have you found to be the primary way that you serve other believers? (Note: We would know this primarily from feedback received rather than merely probing our own motivation.)

---

7. Many have noticed that more often than not the wife, Priscilla, is mentioned first. What could be the significance of this?

---

8. Trace Priscilla and Aquila's ministry to the gifted and influential Apollos (vv. 24-28). What was the context for this ministry?

What was involved in the delicate task of correcting Apollos's understanding?

What were the short-term and long-term (vv. 27-28) results of this service?

9. Many people have suggested that Paul and his friends Priscilla and Aquila could have done a lot more for the kingdom of God and the spread of the gospel if they had allowed themselves to be supported "full time." How would you counter this argument?

---

10. What difference will it make for you to consider your daily work (remunerated or not) and your service to the people of God as part of your calling and your contribution to the kingdom of God?

Thank God for showing that both your work and ministry are sacred. Ask him to help you live that out day by day.

Now or Later

Consider Ephesians 4–6, one of the many Scriptures that point to the comprehensive nature of God's calling (vocation): ministry in the church (Ephesians 4:1-16), mutual service in marriage (Ephesians 5:21-33), service in the home (Ephesians 6:1-4), in the workplace (Ephesians 6:5-9) and in society (Ephesians 6:10-20). What does this mean for your own life?

---

*George MacDonald, *The Curate's Awakening* (Minneapolis: Bethany House, 1985), pp. 189-90.

4

Serving with Heart and Hands

Bezalel and Dorcas

Ministry through our hands? And yet this turns out to be one way we can serve God and neighbor whether we do this as a hobby, as part of domestic life (such as arranging a table with flowers and candles on it), and for some as a full-time occupation that is also a ministry. Craftsmanship involves design, imagination and skill—head, heart and hands united. Crafts are to be distinguished from mass-produced items by machines even though craftsmanship may be involved in the original design, prototypes and the development of the machines themselves. One traditional list of craftspersons includes the artisan, beautician, bookbinder, bricklayer, clock maker, coach builder, barrel maker, coppersmith, currier (leather worker), die sinker, glass blower, gold beater, hairdresser, luthier (maker of stringed instruments), machinist, stonemason, miller, paperhanger, pipe fitter, ceramicist, potter, rigger (of ships), roofer, rope maker, steamfitter, tanner, taxidermist, upholsterer, weaver, welder, window-dresser, woodworker and a wright (someone who repairs something). But this does not cover everything! We could add seamstress, cook, flower arranger, woodcarver and many tasks that are part of everyday homemaking.

GROUP DISCUSSION. Look around the room where you are meeting. Identify those things that were mass-produced and those that were handmade. If the host has made anything in the room or their home, ask him or her to explain what was involved in making it and what it meant.

PERSONAL REFLECTION. When was the last time you made something with your hands? How did you go about it? Did you imagine it first in your mind and then make it? What satisfaction did you have in making it? Did you regard this as a service to yourself (in expressiveness), to a neighbor or even to God? Why?

In this study we consider two passages. The first is the story of Bezalel, a craftsman who is the *only* person in the Old Testament of whom it is definitively said that he was filled "with the Spirit of God." The second is a New Testament early Christian, Dorcas, a woman who was miraculously healed and raised from the dead and was distinguished by her craftsmanship with fabrics. *Read Exodus 35:30–36:7.*

---

1. Bezalel was chosen to make things for the meeting house (tabernacle) for the people of God in the wilderness. What skills did he have (Exodus 35:31-34)?

---

2. What do we learn about Bezalel's natural ability and his personal attitude toward being a craftsman (Exodus 36:2)?

---

3. What do we learn about Bezalel's relationship with Moses and other skilled people? Why are these relationships important?

4. It was obvious for Bezalel and his coworker Oholiab to understand they were serving others and doing this service for the glory of God. Describe any experiences you have had of making something when you have had the same sense of service.

5. What would be the point in this craftsman pair to make *beautiful* things when the sheer functional need could be met more simply?

6. *Read Acts 9:32-43.* What does Peter encounter in his pastoral visitation to the towns of Lydda and Sharon (vv. 32-35)?

7. Describe the ministry of Dorcas (Tabitha) in Joppa before she died.

8. What do we learn about the depth of appreciation people in Lydda had for the craftsmanship of Dorcas?

9. What expectations might the disciples in Joppa have had when they persuaded Peter to come to nearby Joppa, especially in view of what happened to Aeneas (vv. 32-35)?

What did Peter do, and what happened?

10. In these two stories we have encountered people making things by hand that today are usually made by machines (e.g., clothing, jewelry, furniture). Do you agree with Doug Stowe's statement "Without the opportunity to learn through the hands, the world remains abstract, and distant, and the passion for learning will not be engaged?"* Why or why not?

What value do you think taking up a craft can have in your personal life and for society as a whole?

Thank God for making you so that head, heart and hands can be joined in doing something beautiful, useful and pleasing to him.

Now or Later

Consider the following quotation in the light of God the worker (see the notes on question 1) and the role of Adam and Eve as world makers looked at in study 1 on Genesis 1–2.

Commenting on the loss of hands-on work in the so-called information and "creativity" society, the outsourcing of manufacturing (except trades), the disproportionate costs of manufactured goods and handmade goods and the substantial reduction of craftsmanship to hobbies, or specialized work for the wealthy (e.g., custom boat building), Matthew Crawford says, "What is new is the wedding of futurism to what might be called 'virtualism': a vision of the future in which we somehow take leave of material reality and glide about in a pure information economy." Crawford continues, "What if we are inherently instrumental, or pragmatically oriented, all the way down, and the use of tools is really fundamental to the way humans inhabit the world."**

Consider the tools that you use in everyday life (things such as a hammer, cooking utensils, etc.) and make a list of all the tools that enable you to be a craftsperson.

---

*Doug Stowe, quoted in Matthew B. Crawford, *Shop Class as Soulcraft: An Inquiry into the Value of Work* (New York: Penguin, 2009), p. 11.

**Crawford, *Shop Class as Soulcraft*, p. 3.

5

Edifying Others
Through the Arts

David

2 Samuel 6

No one would throw a poem to a person drowning in the water. But what if that person were drowning not in water but in meaninglessness? Then a poem, a work of graphic art, a song, a sculpture or a dance might be just the right thing. But the arts are indirect. They sneak into people's hearts by the back door and surprise people with truth, beauty and joy rather than confronting them bluntly like the direct cannonballs of the prophets. Søren Kierkegaard, the Danish Christian philosopher, constantly used the indirect approach, speaking in parables and pictures, something he found especially effective in a pseudo-Christianized culture. The last book of the New Testament, Revelation, does the same thing, appealing to the prayerful imagination by visions, poems and songs.

GROUP DISCUSSION. Have each person share a particular song, dance, sculpture, film, piece of art or poem that has communicated deeply with them.

PERSONAL REFLECTION. Reflect on your own experience of the arts, possibly trips to an art gallery, an evening at the ballet, an opera, a piece of popular music or a film. What art form speaks most deeply and personally to you? Why?

In this study we are considering only one art form—dance—in a seldom-considered ministry of King David: dancing before the ark of the Lord. But what we learn can apply to all the ways we may use the aesthetic to love and serve our neighbor and bring glory to God: music, graphic arts, scripture, poetry, film and digital media. *Read 2 Samuel 6.*

---

1. In this story David, now king, is bringing the ark of God to Jerusalem; for decades it has been "in exile," captured by Israel's enemies, the Philistines. Describe the two attempts to recover the ark and to bring it to the worship center of Israel, Jerusalem.

---

2. While the text does not tell us in detail why the first attempt failed, and why Uzzah died in the process, what could be some possible reasons?

---

3. Many have suggested that Uzzah arrogantly tried to "save" God and God's holy worship center. How might we as human beings try to manage God and save his church?

---

4. In contrast, in the second attempt to bring the ark, David dances before the parade. What does this tell us about David's spirituality and possible expressions of joy and worship?

5. When have you found yourself expressing beauty or joy through the arts?

6. Many people say things like "I am not very creative" when in fact they do have creative energies and express themselves in an aesthetic way that appeals to the imagination, either their own, that of others or both. Give some examples of this.

7. Michal despises her husband's dancing as a base "show" unfitting for a king. What would cause a person to be so negative about a genuine expression of joy and praise?

How does David deal with his wife, the daughter of Saul?

How does God deal with it?

8. With which of the three main characters—Uzzah, David and Michal—do you find yourself most identifying? Why?

9. How specifically can the arts actually serve our neighbors and God?

10. What difference will this study make in your own expressiveness as a person?

*Tell God he is amazing in revealing himself through so many media and
especially in bodily form in Jesus. Ask him to help you to express yourself,
serve others and bring pleasure to him through some aesthetic expression.*

Now or Later

Dorothy Sayers has suggested that the unique contribution Christianity makes to the arts is that art is not simply a representation of
things that exist but the actual creation of something new. "It is the
artist," she says, "who, more than other men, is able to create something out of nothing. A whole artistic work is immeasurably more
than the sum of its parts."* Here she is not speaking of creating some
thing out of literally no*thing*, but of putting imagination to the task of
creating beauty or new *meaning*.** Give some examples of this.

The following are some further resources in developing a theology
of the arts.***

Rainbows for the Fallen World: Aesthetic Life and Artistic Task by Calvin Seerveld

The Education of Desire: Towards a Theology of the Senses by T. J. Gor-
ringe

"Theology of the Arts and the Vocation of the Artist" by Deborah J.
Haynes, in *Arts* 11, no. 2 (1999)

Michelangelo — "free the angel"

---

*Dorothy L. Sayers, *Christian Letters to a Post-Christian World* (Grand Rapids: Eerdmans, 1969), p. 104.

**Ibid., p. 105.

***I am indebted for some of the preceding to Megan Fowler, my student at Regent
College, for her research and for her paper "Art as Work" (Fall 2011) for the Marketplace Theology course.

6

Helping Friends Find Strength in God

Jonathan

1 Samuel 17:57–18:9;
20:4-42; 23:14-18

In our society friendship is becoming increasingly more difficult. People have lots of relationships. But so many of the relationships are functional—for what people can do for us such as business friends, bridge friends and so on. Real friendship is not "for" anything except the relationship. Further, postmodern culture encourages "openness," which means keeping all your options open "in case something better comes along," not making commitments and more serious still, not making covenants, permanent arrangements of belonging. But friendships are vital to being fully human, to our relationship with God and in being full-time ministers of God. Far from being a hindrance and interruption to our relationship with God, friendships are a major pathway. And a major way we can serve others. Remarkably, Jesus explains his relationship with disciples then and now, as fundamentally one of friendship. "You are my friends" (John 15:14). Lewis Smedes comments on this amazing reality. "To call him friend is not a license to cut him down to our measure of a friend. And yet, in those invisible bonds of moral constancy, kept commitment, gracious forgiveness, untiring listening, and ultimate sacrifice, he is the best friend one can ever have."*

GROUP DISCUSSION. Ask each one in the group to share the person they have had the longest friendship with. Describe that friendship and what it means.

PERSONAL REFLECTION. Take an extended time to review your relational history, friendships from as far back as you can. Then consider your spiritual history, how you came to faith, how you have grown in love of God and neighbor, how you have dealt with issues and temptations, how your service to God and neighbor has grown. And see whether there is a parallel between your relational history and your spiritual history.

In this study we will look at the Old Testament friendship of Jonathan and David (before he became king), and we will see that much of what David became as a king "after God's own heart" is a result of the friendship he had with Jonathan. The same will be true for us. *Read 1 Samuel 17:57–18:9.*

---

1. We begin the study with David as a young man taking up the amazing challenge of fighting and killing Goliath, the Philistine giant, with only five smooth stones and a sling shot. King Saul is impressed. But even more so is Saul's son Jonathan. How does Jonathan express his appreciation of David as a friend?

---

2. David is now in Saul's army and performing spectacularly. While this is not a problem for Jonathan, why is it a problem for King Saul?

3. When, if ever, has the superior performance of another person been a reason to sour your relationship with him or her? What did you do about it, or what came of the relationship?

---

4. *Read 1 Samuel 20:4-42.* Saul's insane jealousy is so dangerous to David that he is on the run for his life as Saul is determined to eliminate the threat. What help does David ask from his friend Jonathan?

---

5. Why would being a loyal friend at this point put Jonathan at risk as the king's son?

---

6. What do we now learn about the depth of relationship between these friends (v. 42)?

---

7. What does it cost Jonathan to be David's friend?

---

8. When, in your experience, has a friendship cost you or your friend deeply?

9. *Read 1 Samuel 23:14-18.* Saul is now desperately trying to wipe out David, his primary threat to his throne, or so he thinks. What specific ministry does Jonathan have with David in this tense situation?

---

10. Why is it so much better to create dependency on God rather than on you as a friend?

---

11. Once again the two friends make a covenant, or more accurately, renew the covenant they have made to stick with and help each other (v. 18). Why do covenants need to be renewed?

---

12. What have you learned from this study that will help you in your ministry to your friends?

Pray to the Lord that you are asking not so much that you may have more friends but that he will help you to be friendly.

Now or Later

"A true friend can never have a hidden motive for being a friend. He can have no hidden agenda. A friend is simply a friend, for the sake of friendship. In a much greater way, love for God is love for God's own sake. Bernard of Clairvaux wrote that our natural inclination is to love for our own sake. When we learn to love God, we still love him for our own sake. As we grow in friendship with God, we come to love him not just for ourselves alone, but also for God's sake. At last, we may reach a point where we love even ourselves for the sake of God."**

To work toward deepening your friendship with someone, get together with him or her and discuss the following questions.

- When did you first experience the warmth of God's love in your life?

- What do you think God is doing in your life now?

- When do you find yourself to be most active in your relationship with God?

- What specific disciplines of the spiritual life have helped you in the past?

- What do you love most in your life?

- Where in your life would you most like God to touch you with insight, healing, comfort and help?

- What do you sense is your next step in drawing closer to God?

---

*Lewis Smedes, "The Sort of Friend We Have in Jesus," in *Perspectives on Christology: Essays in Honor of Paul K. Jewett*, ed. Margaret Schuster and Richard Muller (Grand Rapids: Zondervan, 1991), pp. 241-42.

**James M. Houston, *Transforming Friendship: A Guide to Prayer* (Oxford: Lion, 1989), pp. 195-96.

7

Providing for One's Family

The Entrepreneurial Woman

Proverbs 31:10-31

Tucked away at the end of the Proverbs is this fascinating and challenging picture of service to one's family and beyond. It is challenging because, in answer to the question raised in Proverbs 31:10, "Who can find" such a woman? we might say, "No one!" Some have called Proverbs 31:10-31 one of the "texts of terror" since it describes a superwoman that in comparison with her, other women may feel they pale in significance. But this story follows, first, the tragic humorous picture of the sluggard scattered throughout the Proverbs, and, second, in the Hebrew Bible with the book of Ruth, a truly "noble" woman (Ruth 3:11) who embodied many of the characteristics of the entrepreneurial woman in Proverbs. Then, third, this story is followed in the Hebrew Bible by the Song of Songs, where the beautiful woman is the initiator of an affectionate covenant relationship. So we can view this word picture as an idealized model, not a flesh and blood example. "Not to be used to critique or measure a woman, especially one's wife" should be written in the margin of the Bible. But the picture illuminates an important arena of service in the full-time ministry of all people.

GROUP DISCUSSION. Think of entrepreneurs known to you in business or in a not-for-profit. What are their positive characteristics? What are some of the negative qualities? Do you think you can have one without the other? Why?

PERSONAL REFLECTION. Consider your own work to provide for your family. What specific services do you render for persons important to you? (Single people not living with other family members can ponder what they are doing to provide for others.)

Many of the things described in this study's text—making meals, providing clothing, planning ahead for the needs of the winter season—are very ordinary household chores. In many cases these are done by men as well as women. So it will be important not to let this study become aimed exclusively at women in the group. Homemaking for two-parent families is a joint task. But in reciting such household ministries we are exposed to the way in which ordinary everyday service to our nearest and dearest neighbors—as Martin Luther spoke of his wife and children—is an important ministry. Read Proverbs 31:10-31.

1. What are the inner qualities of this woman (vv. 25-30)?

2. Where might she have acquired these qualities?

3. Entrepreneurship is defined as combining invention or innovation (seeing a possibility or envisioning a new thing) with actual management (making it happen). In what ways do you see this woman combining innovation with management?

4. Have you ever considered that providing for your family is a ministry pleasing to God and uplifting to those closest to you? If so, why and how? If not, why?

---

5. Why do you think providing for one's family is generally not considered an important ministry but just a necessity?

---

6. The entrepreneurial woman has a work ethic that makes her "eager" to work (v. 13), and she works "vigorously" (v. 17) so that she "does not eat the bread of idleness" (v. 27). Where does this come from?

How is this different from workaholism, work addiction?

---

7. The text comments that both the woman's children and her husband call her blessed and praise her (v. 28). In many families this may happen infrequently if at all, especially during certain stages of parenting! What qualities can we cultivate to keep us serving even when that service is not appreciated?

---

8. How is this affected by and nurtured by our relationship with God?

---

9. Why is it an important thing to praise members of your family?

10. Verse 31 says that this remarkable woman is praised "at the city gate" or in the public sphere. Her husband is freed by her industriousness to serve the community where the public business is done at the town gate (v. 23). It is sometimes said that it takes a mature husband to rejoice in the public recognition of his wife's achievements. How is this also an issue of faith and spirituality?

11. What single thing can you apply from this study to your own family relationships?

Thank God for those who have served you in your family. Remember them specifically by name.

Now or Later

Many passages of Scripture describe husband-wife relationships and parent-child relationships as ministry. Read Ephesians 5:21-33 and Ephesians 6:1-4. You may also wish to consider how this much-praised woman represents a radical view on the status and ministry of women that was further advanced by Jesus and the early church. It is worth discussing whether the present view of women in your society and church is more or less advanced than this and why. Be specific for both society and church.

8

Building Unity

Paul

Romans 15:23-33;
1 Corinthians 16:1-4;
2 Corinthians 8:10-15

We live in a fractured world, divided up into races, genders and economic classes with few people building bridges between them. Even in the church, economic and racial groups worship and serve in their own comfortable groups: black, white, rich, poor, blue collar, white collar. Some have said that Sunday morning is the most segregated hour in the week. Some church growth specialists have made a strategy of this situation, arguing that the fastest way to grow a church is to cater to one kind of person, making it a "you all" club where everyone speaks the same way. But is that the church? Not the church of Jesus Christ, which is constituted by a wall broken down by the cross of Christ (Ephesians 2:11-22).

GROUP DISCUSSION. Consider your own church home (or if members of the group come from different churches, you can consider each one). What was the make-up of the first members when the church was formed? What is the composition of the people today? Does your church reflect a particular section of the city, town or community in which they meet?

PERSONAL REFLECTION. Reflect on your own history of relationships. What kinds of people do you find it hardest to relate to, most difficult to like and the most challenging to communicate with? Think of a situation in which you were successful in building a bridge to such a person, and an instance in which you failed.

The apostle Paul is a towering figure in the New Testament known mainly for his frontier-breaking church planting in the Gentile world throughout the Mediterranean. But his deepest passion was not only the expansion of the Christian faith but also building unity between otherwise separated groups of people as they became Christians, especially Jews and Gentiles, who were about as far apart from each other as you can get. In this study we explore Paul's passion and practice of unity-ministry and we will find ways for our own service of building unity between men and women, between rich and poor, and between alienated individuals and groups of people. *Read Romans 15:23-33.*

---

1. Paul is planning to visit the Roman church. The whole letter of Romans is a letter of introduction explaining his grasp of the good news of the kingdom of God. While he is writing from Corinth and is planning to go to Italy he will make a two-thousand-mile detour to Jerusalem carrying a large love gift for the poor saints in the Jewish homeland. What does Paul say are his reasons and hopes for his journey to Rome?

---

2. Paul specifically mentions the money offering he has been collecting from the Gentile churches he has founded and served, an offering he will take personally to Jerusalem. What significance does Paul attach to this large financial blessing?

3. When, if ever, have you been able to use money to build unity, bridge a gap or heal a broken relationship? Explain.

4. What does Paul have in view when he claims he will come in "the full measure of the blessing of Christ" (v. 29) when he finally gets to Rome?

5. *Read 1 Corinthians 16:1-4.* How is this money offering different from much that passes for Christian appeals for the stewardship of your money? How is it similar?

6. *Read 2 Corinthians 8:10-15.* Apparently Paul's first appeal for money from the Corinthians did not produce anything. So he asks again. What does Paul envision as the goal of this project? (Note: the whole of 2 Corinthians 8–9 is devoted to "the collection for the Lord's people.")

7. How does Paul envision this money gift to be a true partnership ("equality," vv. 13-14) and not merely a one-way donation to the poor?

8. What would "equality" of the church in the developing world with the church in the so-called developed world look like?

9. Taking the four Scriptures together (including Ephesians 2:11-22) and the reformulation of the gospel Paul developed for the Gentile world, try to visualize all the ways that Paul attempted to build unity between Jews and Gentiles in Christ.

---

10. How can you build unity in just *one* of the many dimensions of division encountered by New Testament Christians and believers today: men and women; black, brown and white; rich, poor and middle-class; singles and married; educated and uneducated; etc.?

Ask our loving God to help you to be a bridge builder.

Now or Later

Paul's love gift occupies a large part of his correspondence, at least four chapters in total. It appears that while he had originally thought to send to Jerusalem the collected money at the hands of trusted people (1 Corinthians 16:3), he decided in the end to take the money himself—a huge gift, in today's currency perhaps millions of dollars—in time for the feast of Pentecost (Acts 20:16). On the original day of Pentecost people from all the diverse nations were united in Christ (Acts 2:8-12). Perhaps Paul hoped that there would be a renewed Pentecost as a result of this love gift. Scholars have been divided on whether Paul should have spent so much energy raising money and then taking it personally, at great risk as a controversial Christian, to Jerusalem. Some have concluded that "he was out of the will of God."

What do you think?

Using the following Scriptures (and others you might find), build a case for the position that Paul was outside of God's will: Acts 20:16; 21:4, 11; Romans 15:30-32.

Now build a case for the position that Paul was in the will of God: Acts 15:12; 19:21; 21:13; 26:1-2, 22, 30-31; Romans 9:1-5; 10:1, 12-15; Galatians 2:9-10.

What do we learn from this story about doing the will of God?

9

Seeking the Welfare of the City

Erastus

**Jeremiah 29:1-23;
Romans 16:23; Acts 19:21-22;
1 Peter 2:11-12**

"We are all living in exile. Our true homeland is elsewhere." I was with students visiting an orthodox synagogue and Rabbi Martin Hier expressed something of the universal dilemma for people of faith. Our true homeland is the new heaven and new earth, a totally renewed creation. Unfortunately some have interpreted this to mean "this world is not my home, I'm just a-passing through," as the old spiritual put it. But we are not to retreat into a private and personal Christianity that has no concern for social justice or for the culture or city we live in. So part of our service to God and neighbor involves, in the phrase of the prophet Jeremiah writing to exiles in Babylon, "to seek the welfare of the city." God has plans for us right where we are.

GROUP DISCUSSION. Who in your group, or someone known to a group member, has come from a different country to settle where you are? What were some of the experiences of being in a "foreign land?"

PERSONAL REFLECTION. If you have traveled, what was your experience in being in a country where you did not know the language, customs or culture?

In this study we are exploring our service to the city. We do this through three passages of Scripture: first, the long letter of the prophet Jeremiah to the exiles; second, the few cryptic comments in the New Testament about Erastus, who was serving in the church but also was "the city's director of public works" (Romans 16:23), and finally a letter of Peter about how to live in the world. Tragically, the church is often *of* the world without being *in* it, like a boat drawn out of the water but filled with water. *Read Jeremiah 29:1-23.*

---

1. Jeremiah is a prophet of Israel during the troubled time when thousands of citizens had been taken captive and physically transported to Babylon, hundreds of miles away, leaving the poorest of the poor to tend the vines. This is seven centuries before the time of Christ. In contrast to the false prophets in Babylon who were promising a quick return to the homeland, what does Jeremiah say is God's word to them?

False prophets - lying

How long does he say the exile will last, and how should they regard this time of "waiting"?

70 years

---

2. Undoubtedly there was corruption and idolatry in Babylon, not to mention false prophets. How are the people of God to seek the welfare of the city they are living in temporarily?

live normal life; pray to the Lord on its behalf

---

3. Describe the actual situation of your own city or town. Why should you seek its "peace and prosperity" (v. 7)?

In what ways could you individually and corporately as a church contribute to the welfare of your community?

Workship
Echo
Shelter program

4. What faith assurances does Jeremiah give the exiles (vv. 11, 14)?

- God has plans for welfare, a future
- God will restore you

5. Why is it so important for Jeremiah to warn the exiles of false prophets (vv. 15-23)?

a "heads up"

What are false teachers and prophets today telling us about our role in the city? *politicians*

6. *Read Romans 16:23 and Acts 19:21-22. In both church and city, how is the service of Erastus described?*

practical service

7. When you are not meeting with other believers, where are you found in the city?

What difference will it make for you to see this location as providential and an opportunity to seek the welfare of the city?

8. *Read 1 Peter 2:11-12.* How does Peter counsel the believers to whom he writes to live with the tension of "temporarily here" but "destined for a glorious future" just as Jeremiah had done?

Phil 4: 4 - 8

9. What have you learned about serving God where you are even though your ultimate future is elsewhere?

Thank God for all he has done through the history of his people in the world. Ask him to help you take your place in this great service to the city.

Now or Later

It is often said that "Christianity has never done the world any good." The record is actually stunning: the provision of the first hotels, hospices and hospitals; the only people that would bury the dead during plagues; the first burial societies; rescuing abandoned and aborted babies from the garbage heap; bringing dignity and status to women; the first universities; pioneering in health care; strategic help for the poor; microeconomic development; establishing orphanages; the abolition of the slave trade; and so many others.*

List as many biblical and theological reasons as you can for why Christians should take their two-fold service to church and society seriously.

---

*See E. H. Oliver, *The Social Achievements of the Christian Church* (Vancouver: Regent College Publishing, 1930/2004); Stephen Charles Neill and Hans-Ruedi Weber, *The Layman in Christian History* (London: SCM Press, 1963); and Rodney Stark, *For the Glory of God: How Monotheism Led to Reformations, Science, Witch-hunts and the End of Slavery* (Princeton, NJ: Princeton University Press, 2003).

10

Doing Something Beautiful for God

Mary

One of my favorite films is *Babette's Feast*. It is a 1987 award-winning film set in a tiny Jutland village in northern Denmark. It is based on a story written by Isak Dinesen. A French servant, Babette Hersant, working in a strict Protestant home with two very proper sisters, wins the lottery. With this financial windfall she puts together the most amazing feast with imported French wine, quails and everything imaginable for both the family and their religious circle in the village, many of whom were unfamiliar and shocked with the wine and luxurious fare. But Babette's gift breaks down their distrust and superstitions. Old wrongs are forgiven, and around the table there is redemption. The prim and proper sisters assume that the French maid, who used to be chef in the Café Anglaise in Paris, will return home. But she chooses not to, and then informs them that she spent everything on that one feast for a love of these people.

GROUP DISCUSSION. Invite each person to share an extraordinary gift in word or deed they have received, and what it meant to them.

PERSONAL REFLECTION. Consider your record of giving, both in finan-

cial gifts and gifts in kind. When has there been an instance of doing
or giving more than what was considered reasonable? What made
you do it?

The story we are considering in this concluding study is of an extravagant loving service recorded in the second Gospel. The Gospel
of Mark is a succinct story written by a follower of Jesus to introduce
people to the greatest person who has walked across the stage of history. Toward the end of the earthly journey of Jesus of Nazareth,
and sandwiched between the gathering storm of opposition against
Jesus from the teachers of the law and the betrayal of Jesus by his
friend Judas, is this delightful account of Mary's service at a dinner party. There are several Marys in the New Testament, but this is
Mary of Bethany (John 12:2-3), sister of Martha and Lazarus, who
was raised from the dead. In Mark's account of the incident, she is
not named. The action takes place in a home near that of Mary, Martha and Lazarus. Simon the leper is probably a healed friend who
had a larger home for the big event of hosting Jesus and his friends.
Jesus had been spending the days in Jerusalem and the evenings in
Bethany. William Barclay notes that "The poignancy of this story lies
in the fact that it tells us of almost the last kindness Jesus had done
to him."* *Read Mark 14:1-9.*

---

1. In Israel people ate reclining on the floor or cushions. Without
saying a word what does Mary do?

---

2. What does the reaction of the other guests, presumably the male
disciples of Jesus, say about them?

3. When, if ever, have you done something extravagant in service (word or deed) for or to Jesus?

How was it received by those who knew about it?

---

4. The Passover feast, the actual temporal location of this event, was an occasion for giving gifts to the poor. In what way could Mary's act be seen as giving a gift to a poor person?

---

5. Quoting Deuteronomy 15:11 Jesus responds to the indignation of the disciples and friends (v. 7). What does Jesus regard as the disciples' ongoing care of the poor?

How does he regard Mary's service?

---

6. How does Jesus justify and affirm this extravagance?

---

7. In anointing the body of Jesus before his forthcoming burial, what long-term hope is Jesus also proclaiming?

---

8. Martin Luther once said that if your work only serves God and not your neighbor—in his time he viewed the work of monks and nuns as having no benefit to anyone other than themselves and God—then it is *not* good work.** When, if ever, is there a place for doing something beautiful in love, not only *for* God such as in caring for the poor but also *to* God, when God is the only beneficiary?

---

9. Some people have used this story of love's extravagance to justify cathedrals, fabulous church sanctuaries and very expensive religious artifacts. What do you think?

---

10. What are some examples from history of such extravagant service?

---

11. What possible beautiful things could you do for Jesus and to him?

Pray the following prayer: I confess, God, that much of my service has been pinched and stingy. Grant me a generous heart and beautiful service, for your sake.

Now or Later

Review all ten studies. They have covered service in a variety of contexts: family, the physical creation, society, the city, neighbors, relationships, the church and the workplace. We have examined examples of service that were motivated by imagination and a passion inspired by faith, hope or love, or all three. What is the main thing you have learned about being a servant of God and neighbor?

---

*William Barclay, *The Gospel of Mark* (Edinburgh: Saint Andrew Press, 1960), p. 341.

**"If you find a work by which you serve God or His saints or yourself and not your neighbor, know such a work is *not* good." Martin Luther, "Church Postils," in *The Precious and Sacred Writings of Martin Luther* (Minneapolis: Lutherans in All Lands, 1905), 10:27.

Leader's Notes

Leading a Bible discussion can be an enjoyable and rewarding experience. But it can also be *scary*—especially if you've never done it before. If this is your feeling, you're in good company. When God asked Moses to lead the Israelites out of Egypt, he replied, "O Lord, please send someone else to do it!" (Ex 4:13). It was the same with Solomon, Jeremiah and Timothy, but God helped these people in spite of their weaknesses, and he will help you as well.

You don't need to be an expert on the Bible or a trained teacher to lead a Bible discussion. The idea behind these inductive studies is that the leader guides group members to discover for themselves what the Bible has to say. This method of learning will allow group members to remember much more of what is said than a lecture would.

These studies are designed to be led easily. As a matter of fact, the flow of questions through the passage from observation to interpretation to application is so natural that you may feel that the studies lead themselves. This study guide is also flexible. You can use it with a variety of groups—student, professional, neighborhood or church groups. Each study takes forty-five to sixty minutes in a group setting.

There are some important facts to know about group dynamics and encouraging discussion. The suggestions listed below should enable you to effectively and enjoyably fulfill your role as leader.

Preparing for the Study

1. Ask God to help you understand and apply the passage in your own life. Unless this happens, you will not be prepared to lead others. Pray too for the various members of the group. Ask God to open your hearts to the message of his Word and motivate you to action.

2. Read the introduction to the entire guide to get an overview of the entire book and the issues which will be explored.

3. As you begin each study, read and reread the assigned Bible passage to familiarize yourself with it.

4. This study guide is based on the New International Version of the Bible. It will help you and the group if you use this translation as the basis for your study and discussion.

5. Carefully work through each question in the study. Spend time in meditation and reflection as you consider how to respond.

6. Write your thoughts and responses in the space provided in the study guide. This will help you to express your understanding of the passage clearly.

7. It might help to have a Bible dictionary handy. Use it to look up any unfamiliar words, names or places. (For additional help on how to study a passage, see chapter five of *How to Lead a LifeGuide Bible Study,* InterVarsity Press.)

8. Consider how you can apply the Scripture to your life. Remember that the group will follow your lead in responding to the studies. They will not go any deeper than you do.

9. Once you have finished your own study of the passage, familiarize yourself with the leader's notes for the study you are leading. These are designed to help you in several ways. First, they tell you the purpose the study guide author had in mind when writing the study. Take time to think through how the study questions work together to accomplish that purpose. Second, the notes provide you with additional background information or suggestions on group dynamics for various questions. This information can be useful when people have difficulty understanding or answering a question. Third, the leader's notes can alert you to potential problems you may encounter during the study.

10. If you wish to remind yourself of anything mentioned in the leader's notes, make a note to yourself below that question in the study.

Leading the Study

1. Begin the study on time. Open with prayer, asking God to help the group to understand and apply the passage.

2. Be sure that everyone in your group has a study guide. Encourage the group to prepare beforehand for each discussion by reading the introduction to the guide and by working through the questions in the study.

3. At the beginning of your first time together, explain that these studies are meant to be discussions, not lectures. Encourage the members of the group to participate. However, do not put pressure on those who may be hesitant to speak during the first few sessions. You may want to suggest the following guidelines to your group.

☐ Stick to the topic being discussed.

☐ Your responses should be based on the verses which are the focus of the discussion and not on outside authorities such as commentaries or speakers.

☐ These studies focus on a particular passage of Scripture. Only rarely should you refer to other portions of the Bible. This allows for everyone to participate in in-depth study on equal ground.

☐ Anything said in the group is considered confidential and will not be discussed outside the group unless specific permission is given to do so.

☐ We will listen attentively to each other and provide time for each person present to talk.

☐ We will pray for each other.

4. Have a group member read the introduction at the beginning of the discussion.

5. Every session begins with a group discussion question. The question or activity is meant to be used before the passage is read. The question introduces the theme of the study and encourages group members to begin to open up. Encourage as many members as possible to participate, and be ready to get the discussion going with your own response.

This section is designed to reveal where our thoughts or feelings need to be transformed by Scripture. That is why it is especially important not to read the passage before the discussion question is asked. The passage will tend to color the honest reactions people would otherwise give because they are, of course, supposed to think the way the Bible does.

You may want to supplement the group discussion question with an icebreaker to help people to get comfortable. See the community section of *Small Group Idea Book* for more ideas.

You also might want to use the personal reflection question with your group. Either allow a time of silence for people to respond individually or discuss it together.

6. Have a group member (or members if the passage is long) read aloud the passage to be studied. Then give people several minutes to read the passage again silently so that they can take it all in.

7. Question 1 will generally be an overview question designed to briefly survey the passage. Encourage the group to look at the whole passage, but try to avoid getting sidetracked by questions or issues that will be addressed later in the study.

8. As you ask the questions, keep in mind that they are designed to be used just as they are written. You may simply read them aloud. Or you may prefer to express them in your own words.

There may be times when it is appropriate to deviate from the study guide. For example, a question may have already been answered. If so, move on to the next question. Or someone may raise an important question not covered in the guide. Take time to discuss it, but try to keep the group from going off on tangents.

9. Avoid answering your own questions. If necessary, repeat or rephrase them until they are clearly understood. Or point out something you read in the leader's notes to clarify the context or meaning. An eager group quickly becomes passive and silent if they think the leader will do most of the talking.

10. Don't be afraid of silence. People may need time to think about the question before formulating their answers.

11. Don't be content with just one answer. Ask, "What do the rest of you think?" or "Anything else?" until several people have given answers to the question.

12. Acknowledge all contributions. Try to be affirming whenever possible. Never reject an answer. If it is clearly off-base, ask, "Which verse led you to that conclusion?" or again, "What do the rest of you think?"

13. Don't expect every answer to be addressed to you, even though this will probably happen at first. As group members become more at ease, they will begin to truly interact with each other. This is one sign of healthy discussion.

14. Don't be afraid of controversy. It can be very stimulating. If you don't resolve an issue completely, don't be frustrated. Move on and keep it in mind for later. A subsequent study may solve the problem.

15. Periodically summarize what the group has said about the passage. This helps to draw together the various ideas mentioned and gives continuity to the study. But don't preach.

16. At the end of the Bible discussion you may want to allow group members a time of quiet to work on an idea under "Now or Later." Then discuss what you experienced. Or you may want to encourage group members to work on these ideas between meetings. Give an opportunity during the session for people to talk about what they are learning.

17. Conclude your time together with conversational prayer, adapting the prayer suggestion at the end of the study to your group. Ask for God's help in following through on the commitments you've made.

18. End on time.

Many more suggestions and helps are found in *How to Lead a LifeGuide Bible Study.*

Components of Small Groups

A healthy small group should do more than study the Bible. There are four components to consider as you structure your time together.

Nurture. Small groups help us to grow in our knowledge and love of God. Bible study is the key to making this happen and is the foundation of your small group.

Community. Small groups are a great place to develop deep friendships with other Christians. Allow time for informal interaction before and after each study. Plan activities and games that will help you get to know each other. Spend time having fun together going on a picnic or cooking dinner together.

Worship and prayer. Your study will be enhanced by spending time praising God together in prayer or song. Pray for each other's needs and keep track of how God is answering prayer in your group. Ask God to help you to apply what you are learning in your study.

Outreach. Reaching out to others can be a practical way of applying what you are learning, and it will keep your group from becoming self-focused. Host a series of evangelistic discussions for your friends or neighbors. Clean up the yard of an elderly friend. Serve at a soup kitchen together, or spend a day working on a Habitat house.

Many more suggestions and helps in each of these areas are found in *Small Group Idea Book*. Information on building a small group can be found in *Small Group Leaders' Handbook* and *The Big Book on Small Groups* (both from Inter-Varsity Press). Reading through one of these books would be worth your time.

Study 1. Caring for Creation. Genesis 1:26–2:15.
Purpose: To explore the comprehensive service that God calls all human beings to.
Questions 1-2. Participants will need to briefly review the creation account in Genesis 1:1-26. It will be important to stick with the text and not wander off into the debate of creation and evolution, or young earth/old earth debates. The creation story is a marvel of symmetry and order showing how each "day" (whether an eon or a shorter period of time) brings a new "separation" and "filling" to the entire cosmos.

Day 1: light separated	Day 4: lights installed
Day 2: separating space above and below waters	Day 5: filling with fish and fowl
Day 3: dry land and plants	Day 6: filling with land animals and human beings

All this comes about by God speaking. Leon Kass notes "Creation through speech fits creation by separation, for speech implies the making and recognition of distinctions" (Leon Kass, *The Beginning of Wisdom: Reading Genesis* [New York: Free Press, 2003], p. 33).

The use of let us" has resulted in a lot of speculation on whether this is a reference to the triune God (Father, Son and Spirit) or that God is addressing the heavenly angels or a heavenly court. Bruce Waltke affirms the latter. A further, much discussed item, is precisely what is meant by the "image" and "likeness" of God. "Being made in God's image establishes humanity's role on earth and facilitates communication with the divine" (Bruce K. Waltke, *Genesis: A Commentary* [Grand Rapids: Zondervan, 2001], p. 65). In the passage God makes things, God distinguishes things, God names things, and God enjoys things ("It is good"). Clearly the human being is different from the animals in several significant ways, being created to represent the presence and person of God but also as a ruler on earth in place of the deity. The technical word for this is *regent*, who is the person who acts on behalf of a underage or traveling monarch. "Likeness" affirms that while human beings have similarities with God and capacity for knowing God, they are not God. **Question 3.** While it is not until Genesis 3:8 that we learn definitely that God is present in his creation and desires communion with his creatures, we can summarize the human vocation in three dimensions (1) communion with God (worship and dependence); (2) community building (relating to the other sex and building the human community); (3) co-creativity (developing the potential of creation). It will be most helpful if members of the study group can state this in their own words and in the light of their own experience. It may be important to point out that while Christians have tended to define ministry exclusively in terms of the Great Commission in the New Testament (Matthew 28:18-20), that the cultural/creation mandate in Genesis 1 has never been rescinded. Together, the gospel mandate and the creation mandate provide a holistic expression of the ministry and service God desires for himself and his creation.

Question 5. The leader could try out various examples of fulfilling the human vocation to see if they could be considered "ministry": attending to God in prayer and Bible reading; listening to and supporting one's spouse; conceiving children; caring for the needs of one's family; keeping a garden; engaging in work that meets human needs, such as carpentry or financial planning; developing the potential of creation through resource development in mining, forestry and fishing; working for a conservation agency; providing services to other people; creating new products that improve human existence; building global partnerships in business or not-for-profits; helping the poor; working as a volunteer in the church; teaching children in school; and medical service. What difference would it make if these were considered as ministry and that all people are called into full-time ministry?

Question 6. Many Jewish scholars state that the climax of creation is not the sixth day, when man and woman were made, but the seventh—the sabbath. In the New Testament Jesus says the "Sabbath was made for people, not people for the Sabbath" (Mark 2:27). In the Genesis account sabbath is related to God's work: "God's work in one week becomes stamped upon his people as a repeating design for their sanctification" (ibid., p. 71). Later, in Deuteronomy, sabbath is related to redemption (Deuteronomy 5:12-15). The Jewish theologian Abraham Heschel notes how all religions have holy places, but Judaism has sacred *time*. "Spiritual life begins to decay when we fail to sense the grandeur of what is eternal in time" (Abraham Heschel, *The Sabbath: Its Meaning for Modern Man* [New York: Farrar, Straus & Giroux, 1986], p. 3). It will be valuable to draw out what happens (and is happening) in our 24/7 work week without a day of ceasing and celebrating. Sabbath is certainly a cure for workaholism as it affirms that God is

God and our work is not our ultimate concern. Draw out the possibilities of sabbath in our contemporary work life where many in the service sector must work on Saturdays or Sundays (including pastors) and where all too often church activities on Sunday can make that day another work day! Waltke concludes, "In the limitation of God's rest, we find our sustenance in God and the true meaning of our labor and God's good creation" (Waltke, *Genesis*, p. 73).

Question 7. The creation of the man is described as a mixture of dust and divinity. The text describes the man as becoming a "living soul" or a "living being". Waltke explains that the Hebrew word for "soul" (*nephesh*) does not mean a special organ of immortality, as the Greek philosophers argued, but soul means a "passionate vitality," meaning that human beings have a passion appetite for food, sex and God (ibid., p. 71). Put this way our human soul sets us apart from animals, who also have drives for food and sex, but are not set apart with a hunger for God. "We are to be distinguished by our godlike compassion in connection with our ruling. Like God, we are to be merciful kings" (ibid.).

In the creation of the woman the first word of judgment in the Bible is "It is not good for the man to be alone" (Genesis 2:18)—judging man's solitariness. We are made for community. So God creates a desire for a companion by getting Adam to name all the animals (Genesis 2:20). Derek Kidner notes, "The naming of the animals, a scene which portrays man as monarch of all he surveys, poignantly reveals him as a social being, made for fellowship, not power; he will not live until he loves, giving himself away to another on his own level. So the woman is presented wholly as his partner. . . . She is valued for herself alone" (Derek Kidner, *Genesis: An Introduction and Commentary* [Downers Grove, IL: InterVarsity Press, 1977], p. 65). God makes a creature that is equal and adequate to himself—the true meaning of "helper suitable" (Genesis 2:18) and like the father of the bride brings the man to the woman. Then follows the first hymn of praise in the Bible, a song of relational joy: "This is now . . ." (Genesis 2:23).

Question 8. Of significant note is that work was given before the Fall into sin. It is a gift of God, not a punishment for wrongdoing. The phrase *take care of* is used for the activity of priests. The thought that human beings are priests of creation is developed wonderfully by Alexander Schmemann: "The first, the basic definition of man is that he is a *priest*. He stands in the center of the world and unifies it in his act of blessing God, of both receiving the world from God and offering it to God—and by filling the world with this eucharist [thanksgiving], he transforms his life, the one that he receives from the world, into life in God, into communion with Him" (Alexander Schmemann, *For the Life of the World: Sacraments and Orthodoxy* [Crestwood, NY: St. Vladimir's Seminary Press, 1988], p. 15).

The command to "fill the earth" certainly includes procreation and populating the planet, but it also means filling the earth with the glory of God. This "filling" is something the men and women of Babel refused to do (Genesis 11:1-9), but were forced to do. Later, it was fulfilled in the coming of Jesus both in his first coming and his sending the Spirit to "fill the whole universe" (Ephesians 4:10) and finally in the global mission of the people of God (Acts 2:1-21).

Significantly God calls everything he made "good," meaning fitted for the purpose and beautiful, except the human being. What significance does the "tree of the knowledge of good and evil" (Genesis 2:9) have in the possibility of human beings becoming good? (Genesis 3 tells the story of the man and woman's failure to be good and the beginning of God's recovery operation.)

Question 9. Elsbeth Martens, reviewing Robert Capon's *An Offering of Uncles*, says that "Capon rescues the earthly world from the clutches of a skinny and miserly dualism [that some things are sacred and others are secular]. . . . This willingness on God's part to allow us to shape history and yet still have it come out how he wants is an example of his supreme sovereignty and mystery" (Elsbeth Martens, "A Review of An Offering of Uncles," unpublished paper, Regent College, Vancouver, 2012).

Study 2. Witnessing About Jesus. John 4:1-42.

Purpose: To learn how relationships are the natural context for sharing the gospel.

Question 1. Note the disconnect between Jesus' statements and what the woman is hearing. He is offering living water (water that flowed, in contrast with still or stagnant water) but on a deeper level he is offering overflowing abundant life (see John 1:4; 3:15). "It is much more than merely the entrance into a new state, that of being saved instead of lost. It is the abundant life (10:10)" (Leon Morris, *The Gospel According to John* [Grand Rapids: Eerdmans, 1971], p. 263). Drinking living water was a longstanding biblical promise—drawing water with joy from the well of salvation (Psalm 42:1; Isaiah 12:3; 44:3). William Barclay notes "there are few stories in the Gospel record which show us so much about the character of Jesus as this story does" (William Barclay, *The Gospel of John* [Edinburgh: Saint Andrew Press, 1963], p. 140). He notes the reality of his humanity, the warmth of his sympathy, his determination to break down barriers (including religious custom) and his respect of women. "When Jesus spoke about bringing to men the water which quenches thirst for ever, He was doing no less than stating that He was the Anointed One of God who was to bring the new age in" (Barclay, *Gospel of John*, p. 146).

Question 2. The Gospel of John presents Jesus in a unique way through his signs (miracles and self-revelations), his words and finally his death and resurrection. All four Gospels are a new form of literature created by the early disciples to present Jesus and Jesus' gospel of the kingdom of God. John, the fourth Gospel, is, as some have commented, so simple that it is like a pool a child could wade in, and yet so deep that an elephant could swim in it. The passage is rich in revealing Jesus as a human being, his needs, his initiative taking and his love. The introductory verses in the passage (vv. 1-4) note the fact that more people were becoming disciples of Jesus than John the Baptist had. It seems that to avoid a premature clash with the Pharisees before his "time" was right for his public revelation and consequent crucifixion (something which this Gospel writer notes elsewhere), Jesus decided to leave the epicenter of Jewish religion and head north for Galilee. Unlike most strict Jews who would avoid going through the hated Samaritan area, and consequently would take a longer route on the other side of the Jordan, Jesus is determined to take that route. Jacob's well is rich in biblical history. It is on a piece of land bought by Jacob (Genesis 33:18-19), who on his deathbed had bequeathed the ground to Joseph for his burial (Joshua 24:32). Noting that Jesus was tired, hungry and thirsty is the writer's witness to the full humanity of Jesus. Later his full divinity will be declared.

Question 3. The hostility of the Jews toward the Samaritans goes a long way back. During the deportation of the northern people (then they went by the title "Israel") to Assyria, the Assyrians replaced the deportees with their own citizens, who brought their own gods and mixed it with Yahweh worship. Eventually the ensuing polytheism disappeared but the remaining Jews only honored the first five books of the Bible as Scripture (the Pentateuch), thus ignoring the prophets, history, psalms and writings. They did not worship in Jerusalem but built their own temple on Mount Gerizim around 400 B.C., though this temple was burned before the time of Christ. The feelings that existed between the Jews and the "half-Jews" in Samaria is summarized by the words of Ben Sira in Ecclesiasticus: "With two nations my soul is vexed, and the third is no nation: those who live on Mount Seir and the Philistines, and the foolish people that dwell in Shechem" (Sirach 50:25-26, quoted in Morris, *Gospel According to John*, p. 256). It is not clear why the woman was at the well in midday, when the usual time was late in the day, but it may have been her desire not to meet other women because she had such a bad reputation. But there was a further surprise: Jesus was talking with a woman in public!

Question 4. Godet remarks on this, "He is not unaware that the way to gain a soul is often to ask service of it" (F. L. Godet, quoted in Morris, *Gospel According to John*, p. 258). In the light of the fact that Jews did not even use utensils of Samaritans, Jesus' action in asking for help to get water, as he did not have a vessel, was all the more remarkable. The well was about one hundred feet deep, and without a bucket one could not drink. The Jewish Mishnah (a commentary on Scripture) states, "The daughters of the Samaritans are (deemed unclean as) menstruants from their cradle" (Mishnah, *Niddah*

4.1, quoted in Morris, *Gospel According to John*, p. 259). Eating bread with a Samaritan was like eating the flesh of swine, says another regulation in Jewish life.

Question 5. The woman is thinking of her own convenience—not having to come back every day to the well. Until she knows and admits her neediness she will not be able to have the abundant life Jesus offers. The fathers and mothers of the church, and notably the theologian John Calvin, have repeatedly affirmed that true religion is to know God and to know ourselves. But by "knowing ourselves" they do not mean self-realization in the postmodern sense, but knowing how needy we are. Teresa of Ávila, the medieval Carmelite nun and reformer said, "Self-knowledge is so important that, even if you were raised right up to the heavens, I should like you never to relax your cultivation of it; so long as we are on this earth, nothing matters more to us than humility." She continues, "As I see it, we shall never succeed in knowing ourselves unless we seek to know God. . . . By looking at His purity we shall see our foulness" (Teresa of Ávila, *Interior Castle*, trans. E. Allison Peers [New York: Doubleday, 1989], p. 38).

Question 6. The right place to worship God was a disputed issue for the Jews. For the Samaritans Mount Gerizim had traction as the right place. In Deuteronomy it was a place of blessing for the people (Deuteronomy 11:29; 27:12), and it was commanded to have an altar there (Deuteronomy 27:4-8). But there was a problem. Goodspeed paraphrases, "You worship something you know nothing about" (quoted in Morris, *Gospel According to John*, p. 270). But for Jesus, genuine worship is spiritual and does not depend on a special place but is a matter of spirit (probably not the Spirit) and truth (something the woman was being confronted with) (see Zephaniah 2:11; Malachi 1:11). But it is also a matter of the Father's seeking initiative. The woman wants to know, "Where can I find God?" and the answer Jesus gives is "Right where you are" (Barclay, *Gospel of John*, p. 150). The statement that "salvation is from the Jews" is seen to be problematic, but all the promises of the Messiah suggested that the Messiah had to be a Jew, not a Samaritan. But when Jesus finally discloses himself—"I, the one speaking to you am—I am he" (v. 26), he is more than either a Jew or Samaritan could comprehend.

Question 7. William Barclay describes what good news it is to have a Savior. "A great example can be merely a heart-breaking and frustrating thing when we find ourselves powerless to follow it. Jesus was *Saviour*. That is to say, He rescued men from the evil and hopeless situation in which they found themselves; He broke the chains that bound them to the past and gave them power and a presence which enabled them to meet the future. The Samaritan woman is in fact the great example of His saving power. The town where she stayed would no doubt have labelled her a character beyond reformation; and she herself would no doubt have agreed that a respectable life was beyond her. But Jesus came and He doubly rescued her; He enabled her to break away from the past and He opened a new future to her. There is no title adequate to describe Jesus except the Saviour of the World" (ibid., pp. 165-66).

Question 8. It is truism, largely unappreciated, that Jesus did not preach the gospel of personal salvation but rather the good news of the kingdom of God (Mark 1:15), something which includes soul salvation but involves the shalom-bringing rule of God in all of life. For Jesus to say that he has come to do the will of the Father and that this is his meat and drink is to affirm that he embodies the kingdom or rule of God in his own person and that his actions and final self-giving on the cross would bring in the kingdom substantially. Preoccupation with the Great Commission (Matthew 28:18-20) has short-circuited many believers from the "greatest commission" in John 20:21: "As the Father has sent me, I am sending you" in a fully incarnational mission with all the resources of the triune God. Consequently Jesus not only preached but healed and addressed the principalities and powers of his day. The remarks of Jesus about "sowing and reaping" (vv. 35-38) may encourage some discussion on whether we are "sowers" or "reapers," though clearly Jesus expects his immediate disciples to be reapers. Is that true of all believers today or only of those who have a special gift of evangelism?

Question 9. The townspeople "hear for themselves" and did not simply take the woman's witness as their own. This surely is the ultimate challenge in witnessing to Jesus. How can we make the self-revelation of Jesus to people happen? Hearsay is not good enough. Jesus addresses the same issue and provides a wonderful answer when he has the disciples on a retreat: "Who do you say I am?" (Matthew 16:13-20). Bernard of Clairvaux gives us a signal of what that could look like. He writes, "Every soul among you that is seeking God will know that he has gone before you and sought you before you sought him" (Bernard of Clairvaux, *Bernard of Clairvaux: Selected Works*. ed. Emilie Griffin, HarperCollins Spiritual Classics [San Francisco: HarperSanFrancisco, 2005], p. 128). In other words, we would not be seeking God if we had not already been found by him.

Study 3. Building Up the People of God. Acts 18:18-28.

Purpose: To discover how daily work and church ministry can both be service to God and neighbor.

Question 1. Paul's missionary journeys can be traced on a good map of the Mediterranean. His first journey took him from Antioch to Cyprus, then to ancient Asia Minor (modern Turkey) to Perga, Lystra and Pisidian Antioch and back. The second, leaving from Caesarea to Galatia (northern Turkey) then went into Europe—Philippi, Thessalonica, Athens, Corinth—and then back through Asia Minor by way of Ephesus. The third missionary journey starts in Antioch, goes through Galatia, returning to the new churches in

Europe and then back through the Greek Islands, Ephesus and on to Jerusalem. This account is largely from the second and third missionary journeys.

We do not know what the nature of the vow Paul made in Cenchrae (v. 18). But his cutting off his hair on this and on a later occasion (Acts 21:22-24) makes it apparent that Paul functions as a Jew among Jews and a Gentile among Gentiles without compromising his faith. Most likely this was a short-term Nazirite vow (Numbers 6:1-21) by which one would cut his hair for the period and burn the hair along with other sacrifices as a symbol of self-offering to God. Paul may have had in mind his desire to conciliate the Jewish Christian leaders in Jerusalem, where he was going (John R. W. Stott, *The Spirit, the Church and the World: The Message of Acts* [Downers Grove, IL: InterVarsity Press, 1990], pp. 300-301).

Question 2. The places in the New Testament where Aquila and Priscilla are named are Acts 18:2, 18, 26; Romans 16:3; 1 Corinthians 16:19; and 2 Timothy 4:19. Their trade was sewing tents from rough cloth woven from goat's hair or leather, a very portable trade enabling them to sell their wares in almost any marketplace. The apostle Paul worked alongside this couple supporting his own apostolic ministry by a trade, as was common with all rabbis, though from time to time he received financial support and patronage from distant churches (2 Corinthians 11:9; Philippians 4:10-20). Tentmaking is a pattern of relating work and ministry so that both are for God's glory. The tentmaker thus has a second major arena of service in addition to the workplace. The great danger of this arrangement is that someone will regard his or her work as merely the means of making a livelihood rather than an arena of co-creativity, mission and caretaking of God's world (Genesis 2:15). Tents (or some modern equivalent) should be made not only to gain access to a closed society but also for God's glory and people's use. So the true tentmaker witnesses in his or her work, not just working in order to be positioned to witness.

Question 3. The teaching that some activities for Christians, such as daily work, is "secular" and other activities, such as teaching Sunday school, is sacred, is the most pervasive and destructive heresy in the worldwide church. For the New Testament Christian all of life is sacred (Romans 12:1-2) and all aspects of everyday life are presented to God as a living sacrifice. Tragically this sacred-secular divide (dualism) is institutionalized in much of the church with the clergy-laity distinction, a hierarchy of holiness that was eliminated by Jesus and the outpouring of the Spirit on the church (see R. Paul Stevens, *Liberating the Laity* [Vancouver: Regent College Publishing, 1969]; and R. Paul Stevens, *The Other Six Days: Vocation, Work and Ministry in Biblical Perspective* [Grand Rapids: Eerdmans, 1999]).

Question 4. Tentmakers are determined not to be a burden to the people they serve. Undoubtedly Paul's daily work was arduous. It was not peripheral but central to his daily life. Tentmakers set an example. Paul undertook a tentmaking lifestyle as an example to others of priorities and balance in ministry. In Ephesus his working from early dawn to mid-evening demonstrated his generosity: "In everything I did, I showed you that by this kind of hard work we must help the weak, remembering the words the Lord Jesus himself said: 'It is more blessed to give than to receive'" (Acts 20:35). Like Jesus, Christian leaders come not to be ministered to but to serve, not to receive but to give. Paul believed that his tentmaking approach helped the weak in faith, who frequently imagine that their next step in discipleship is to be supported financially by other Christians.

Question 5. In Romans 16:3-5 Paul asks the Roman Christians to greet Priscilla and Aquila and "the church that meets in their house." Most churches in the first 250 years were house churches, gatherings of 12-50 in the atrium of a larger home and composed of people who dispersed to work and serve in the world. Of the latter is the example of the biblical character Erastus, the director of the city's public works (Romans 16:23) to be considered later. Often when they gathered, there was a shared meal and the Eucharist/Communion would have been part of a real meal, not a wafer and a sip of wine (Acts 2:42-47). Ministry was not vested in one person but shared in the community with people bringing a hymn, a Scripture, a lesson or story, a prayer and an exhortation or prophecy. First Corinthians 12–14 gives us some of the dimensions of that shared life, as well as problems that can emerge. Some will note that house churches were very similar to the contemporary experience of small groups or Bible studies in homes, except for the lack of the Lord's Supper and a sermon or prophecy. By and large, contemporary churches reserve worship for Sunday services, something which New Testament Christians would have found strange in that their whole life was worship. They gathered for edification, building one another up in faith and life. Bruce Winter notes that "'Edification' was a unique term which Paul coined for the Christian faith which reflects the responsibility individuals should assume for the welfare of others as a matter of 'religious' obligation" (Bruce W. Winter, *Seek the Welfare of the City: Christians as Benefactors and Citizens* [Grand Rapids: Eerdmans, 1994], p. 175). To facilitate this in the present situation is something the group may wish to discuss.

Question 6. This question is quite personal and possibly even a little dangerous. Many people have a desire for certain kinds of ministry, often the ones given most accolades in the church, such as preaching or music leadership, when their real gift for ministry lies in another direction. Some groups have found it helpful to reserve part of an evening or even a whole evening to affirming the service of its members. This is best done not by trying to designate someone's "gift," which could put someone in a box, but by finishing the sentence, "In our group God seems to work through you in . . ." Two or three people could respond to each member. Sometimes people speak of "spiritual gifts" as something quite unrelated to the capacities that God built into a person in creation. To this G. Campbell Morgan says, "The Spirit always bestows His special gift upon a man already gifted by nature to receive it" (G. Campbell Morgan, *The Acts of the Apostles* [Westwood, NJ: Fleming H. Revell, 1924], p. 438). Such a person was Apollos, who knew "only the baptism and teaching of John the Baptist." Morgan says, "One of the most beautiful touches about Apollos is the revelation of the fact that he was willing to let two members of the congregation who listened to him, and who knew more than he did, teach him. They took him, this persuasive, eloquent, burning soul; and opened to him the truth, with the result he passed on from Ephesus to Corinth" (ibid., p. 440). The effect of this is mentioned in 1 Corinthians 3:6.

Question 7. It is possible that Priscilla was the natural leader of the Aquila and Priscilla team. The New Testament does witness to women taking leadership in churches, notably Lydia, the textile merchant who hosted a church in her home (Acts 16:11-15, 40). There is no point in strong women pretending they are weak in the church when the church can benefit from their strength.

Question 8. Members of the study group can be encouraged to share a situation in which they were personally corrected, as Apollos was in this story, by another believer. Have them share what medium was used: email, text, letter or face to face, and how they felt about this challenge. Was it public or private? A helpful guideline that someone has proposed is this: email and texting only for the transmission of information, telephone when decisions have to be made (when you can respond and hear the tone of voice), but discipline should only be undertaken face to face. The relative anonymity of the Internet allows people to say things in a way they never would face to face and often with devastating effect. F. F. Bruce notes, "How much better it is to give such private help to a preacher whose ministry is defective than to correct or denounce him publicly!" (F. F. Bruce, quoted in Stott, *The Spirit, the Church and the World*, p. 302).

Questions 9-10. It is often missed in the Gospels that Jesus did not preach the gospel of soul salvation but the gospel of the kingdom of God, God's life-giving rule brought into the world and into the whole of people's lives. Kingdom work creates new wealth, improves human life, brings God's shalom into the world and invites people to bring their personal lives under the lordship of Jesus. Leland Ryken says "Any job that serves humanity and in which one can glorify God is a Kingdom job" (Leland Ryken, *Work and Leisure in Christian Perspective* [Eugene OR: Wipf & Stock, 1987], p. 136). The English reformer William Tyndale said, "There is no work better than another to please God; to pour water, to wash dishes, to be a souter (cobbler), or an apostle, all are one, as touching the deed, to please God" (William Tyndale, "A Parable of the Wicked Mammon," in *Doctrinal Treatises and Portions of Holy Scripture* [Cambridge: Parker Society, 1848], pp. 98, 104).

Some have said that if Christians said nothing for a year but did their daily work for God (Colossians 3:22–4:1) that perhaps more people would become Christians, attracted by the witness of their work. So, as something to discuss, should we eliminate reserving the term *full-time* for supported Christian workers and keep the term for all believers? Along the same line, as we learned in the first study, everyone doing good work is doing "the Lord's work." Easily said. The reality of it, as Luther once said about justification by faith through grace, is something we have to beat into our heads every day.

Study 4. Serving with Heart and Hands. Exodus 35:30–36:1; Acts 9:32-43.
Purpose: To discover how each of us serves others through some form of craftsmanship, whether as remunerated work or part of everyday life through the involvement of the whole person: head, heart and hands.
Questions 1-2. The range of skills enjoyed by Bezalel was truly extraordinary: craftsmanship in fabric, gems and metals. Then, in addition, he had the ability to teach others. The list of internal qualities in Exodus 35:31 suggests that he had passion and desire to do this work, and practical knowledge of how to do it, all at the initiative of God. There are important clues in this passage of how to discern one's vocation. Frederick Buechner is famously quoted as saying, "The place God calls you to is the place where your deep gladness and the world's deep hunger meet" (Frederick Buechner, *Wishful Thinking: A Theological ABC* [New York: Harper & Row, 1973], p. 95). Mark Twain said something similar: "'Blessed is the man who has found his work'? Mark you, he says *his* work—not somebody else's work. The work that is really man's own work is play and not work at all" (Mark Twain, "A Humorist's Confession," *New York Times*, November 26, 1903, quoted in Ben Witherington III, *Work: A Kingdom Perspective on Labor* [Grand Rapids: Eerdmans, 2011], p. 14). This story is a powerful illustration of the principle that the Holy Spirit inspires us with wisdom, discernment and skill to make good and beautiful things in the world, and he makes it clear what we are called to be and do by writing God's will into the fibers of our lives.

We discovered in the first study that human beings are creative creatures, made in the image of God. In the Bible the first artisan is God—the worker who makes things with imagination, creativity, with both form and function. God is composer and performer, metalworker and potter, garment maker and dresser, gardener and orchardist, farmer and winemaker, shepherd and pastoralist, tentmaker and camper, builder and architect (see Robert Banks, *God the Worker: Journeys into the Mind, Heart and Imagination of God* [Valley Forge, PA: Judson Press, 1992]).

Question 3. Moses is clearly in charge of the process and has been directed by God with the overall plan as well as the selection of Bezalel. This raises the important question of affirmation by others and accountability to others in choosing a vocational expression, something not often recognized in an individualistic and self-realizing culture. Exodus 36:2 notes that Bezalel and Oholiab's helpers were essentially volunteers. Their hearts were lifted up to become involved in the work.

Question 4. The leader of the group should draw out from the group concrete examples of making things and the feelings, perspectives and possible God-inspired joy in doing so. Most will be surprised that even though our lives are filled with mass-produced articles, we still engage in crafts. And if not, why not? It is important for every human being to be making something!

Question 5. One of the things we learn from both Testaments is that good work not only meets a basic human need in our neighbor but also improves human life or embellishes human existence. This is a classic example. In some translations Exodus 28:2 describes how God instructed Moses to have sacred priestly garments made "for glory and for beauty" ("to give him dignity and honor"). The study group may wish to respond to the proposal that beauty is not just in music and graphic art, but in a meal or a deal, a voice or an invoice, an operation or a cooperation, a community formed or an immunity created, a test or a quest, a canvas painting or a computer program, a toy or a tool.

Question 6. It is apparent that Peter was not only preaching the gospel in his traveling but also visiting and encouraging believers. In this double incident he is next to the seashore visiting two towns, Joppa (modern Jaffa) and Lydda, twelve miles southeast.

Question 9. John Stott notes four reasons why the ministry of Peter verifies that he is a true apostle of Jesus Christ. First, he follows the example of Jesus, who healed the paralyzed man by the pool, who also had to "take up his mat" and walk, and Jesus raised Jairus's daughter, using a similar phrase, "*Talitha koum*" (young woman get up) almost identical to the words Peter used: "*Tabitha koum*." Second, both miracles were accomplished by the power of Jesus (v. 34). Third, both miracles were signs of holistic salvation. The use of "Get up" (vv. 34, 40) is reminiscent of the resurrection of Jesus. Finally, both miracles brought glory to God as many people in both towns came to the Lord.

Question 10. Crafts serve a societal function. They are an expression of culture, preserving important cultural artifacts. Crafts serve a personal function in helping to reintegrate the person—body, soul and spirit (especially for knowledge workers and professionals). Crafts serve a spiritual function in being God work (sub- or co-creativity) that is worshipful, spiritually invigorating and edifying to others.

Study 5. Edifying Others Through the Arts. 2 Samuel 6.

Purpose: To revel in the God-given capacity each person has to express something artistically.

Question 1. The ark was captured by the Philistines (1 Samuel 4–7) during a battle, but it brought so much hardship on them that they wanted to get rid of it. So they sent it on a cart into Israel's territory, first to Beth Shemesh and then to Kiriath Jearim. By some estimates this was over a period of about seventy years (C. F. Keil and F. Delitzsch, *Commentary on the Old Testament*, vol. 2, *Joshua, Judges, Ruth, I & II Samuel*, trans. James Martin [Grand Rapids: Eerdmans, n.d.], p. 330). But even in Israel territory the presence of the ark proved to be dangerous, with some people dying in association with it. So it sat there for decades. Meanwhile David became king and wanted to bring the ark home. The chapter describes two attempts and three responses: the abortive attempt of David with the death of Uzzah, the successful attempt of David with his leading the procession with dance, and the despising of David's dance by his wife, Michal.

Question 2. The passage unfortunately does not tell us exactly why, when he tried to keep the ark from falling on to the ground, Uzzah was struck dead. As Eugene Peterson notes, "It is difficult to fit this episode into our picture of the God who is consistently revealed as the giver of life, patiently calling us to repentance, constantly seeking the lost, undeflected in his steadfast love for us" (Eugene H. Peterson, *Leap Over a Wall: Earthy Spirituality for Everyday Christians* [San Francisco: HarperSanFrancisco, 1997], p. 149). Peterson compares this story with the death of Ananias and Sapphira in Acts 5. They had misrepresented their gift to the church deceptively and were struck dead, though in those vital first years of the church it may have been a choice between dead liars or a dead church. Both the Old Testament story of Uzzah and the New Testament story of Ananias and Sapphira tell us that the true fear of God—reverent awe and affection—prevents death by religion. Eric Rust suggests that "Uzzah may have been paralyzed and even struck dead by the fear aroused when he touched the holy object. Similar reactions still occur today among primitive peoples and are exploited by witch doctors" (Eric C. Rust, *Judges–Samuel*, Layman's Bible Commentary 6 [Atlanta Georgia: John Knox Press, 1961], p. 130).

Question 3. One thing we know from the Old Testament is that the ark was a sacred thing that should be touched only by the priests and carried not on a cart but slowly by the Levites on foot using poles slipped through rings on each side. So now, not just the Philistines but even the people of God were using modern technology, a cart and oxen, to get the job done efficiently—a motorized worship center. Peterson joins centuries of imaginative reconstruction to suggest that "Uzzah was the person who has God in a box and officiously assumes responsibility for keeping him safe from the mud and dust of the world. . . . Holy Scripture posts Uzzah as a danger sign for us: 'Beware the God.' . . . If we think and act as he did, we'll be dead men and women, soon or late" (Peterson, *Leap Over a Wall*, pp. 150-51).

Question 4. After Uzzah died David was angry with God. This is not the same as despising God. Indeed, the psalms are full of David's and other leaders' complaints against God. The psalms reveal a God we can pour out our heart to, just the way we feel. David made a temporary arrangement for the ark in the house of Obed-Edom, a Gittite, and learning that the family had been blessed with the presence of the ark David decided once more to bring the ark to Jerusalem. This time the ark was moved the correct way, by Levites carrying it (v. 13). David is so joyful that he stripped down to a simple tunic and danced at the front of the procession to the tune of trumpets and shoutings, becoming one of the people in humility. (Keil and Delitzsch claim the tunic was a linen ephod, a shoulder dress, that would normally be worn by Levites, and that Michal's criticism of David was doubly focused, his dressing like a Levite, a person she despised, and his acting as one of the people [Keil and Delitzsch, *Commentary on the Old Testament*, p. 338].) Peterson comments, "In God, David had access to life that exceeded his capacity to measure and control. He was on the edge of mystery, of glory. And so he danced" (Peterson, *Leap Over a Wall*, p. 152). This scene is a counterpoise with much that passes for religion: controlled, sedate, packaged, predictable, inoffensive and innocuous services of worship that inoculate people from the real thing—a whole person expressively abandoned to the beauty and glory of God.

Question 5. One thing that the Bible does not do is to forbid artistic expression. Indeed it positively encourages aesthetic expression. The reason is profoundly theological. God is an artist, a musician and a dancer in the love communion of the Holy Trinity: Father, Son and Spirit in the dance of unity through diversity. We also saw in study one that humankind was made like God, indeed made out of the imagination of God who saw us in his mind's eye before he painted us, heard us as a melody before he sang us into existence and composed us as a poem before he wrote us down. Human beings also make things twice, first in the inner world of their imaginations and then in the outer world. So aesthetics is part of what it means to be human. The trees in the Garden in Eden were "good for food" and a "delight to the eyes," all of which was to be enjoyed in communion with God. The three temptations of leisure revealed in Genesis 3:6 are godless sensuality (good for food), a godless aesthetic (delight to the eyes) and godless experience (desired to make one wise and independent). While these are temptations that exist throughout the ages, it is clear that God means human beings to enjoy God's creation, to delight in beauty and to thrive. Part of human thriving, and our ministry to neighbors, is the artistic creation of beauty, even when no discernible functional value exists.

Question 7. Peterson comments, "For Michal, God had become a social amenity, a political backer. Michal was first embarrassed by and then contemptuous of David's dance. I've always liked Alexander Whyte's sentence on Michal: 'Those who are deaf always despise those who dance'" (Peterson, *Leap Over a Wall*, p. 153). Michal was subsequently unable to have children, and so the house of Saul was not continued through the house of David.

Study 6. Helping Friends Find Strength in God. 1 Samuel 17:57—18:9; 20:4-42; 23:14-18.

Purpose: To explore the ministry of friendship.

Question 1. It may be valuable for the group leader to review the story of David's successful contest with Goliath because several factors are not always well-known (1 Samuel 17): Goliath's challenge to a singlehanded dual rather than an army versus army; David as the youngest son visiting his brothers back and forth on the battlefield bringing food; David's brothers despising their younger brother for taking an interest in the dual; David meeting Saul and offering to take on the giant; David's refusal to be encumbered with Saul's armor and electing to choose a method he knew well—stones and a sling shot; David's challenge to Goliath and Goliath's rebuke; David's trust that God could give him victory; David's success in killing the giant.

Question 2. Eugene Peterson reflects on King Saul in terms of Saul's relationship with God: "The opportunism with which Saul had earlier treated God is reproduced in opportunism with regard to David. Just as God had become an auxiliary appendage to Saul's royal ego, to be used but not obeyed, so David is now valued only because he is useful for musical solace and military prowess" (ibid., p. 52). David's growing friendship with Jonathan is critical to his training to be king of Israel. Keil and Delitzsch comment on the fruits of the friendship: "This friendship on the part of the brave and noble son of the king, not only helped David to bear the more easily all the enmity and persecution of the king when plagued by his evil spirit, but awakened and strengthened in his soul that pure feeling of unswerving fidelity towards the king himself, which amounted even to love of his enemy, and, according to the marvellous counsel of the Lord, contributed greatly to the training of David for his calling to be a king after God's own heart" (C. F. Keil and F. Delitzsch, *Commentary on the Old Testament,* vol. 3, *Joshua-Samuel,* trans. James Martin [Grand Rapids: Eerdmans, 1988], p. 186).

Questions 2-3. Many leaders have a fatal flaw that is frequently represented in Shakespeare's plays. Failure to deal with it often leads to a stunning downfall. Saul seems to have an inferiority complex and was profoundly insecure. But it was not simply a psychological problem but one relating to his faith. Saul functions as king without any personal relationship with God. People who are secure and approved in God, such as the servant in Isaiah

42:1-9, are able to welcome and prize the strength and giftedness of others, especially those who are serving with them or under them. Carlo Carretto speaks of this "fatal flow" eloquently:

> In the depths lodges the most crucial fault, greater than any other though it is hidden. It rarely, or perhaps never, breaks out in single concrete actions pushing toward the surface of the world. But from the depths, from the inmost layers of our being, it soaks in a poison which causes extreme damage. . . . Because it is hidden, or camouflaged, we can barely catch sight of it, and often only after a long time; but it is alive enough in our consciousness to be able to contaminate us and it weighs us down considerably more than the things we habitually confess. . . . They burden our whole existence and damage it. (Carlo Carretto, *Letters from the Desert*, trans. Rose Mary Hancock [Maryknoll, NY: Orbis Books, 2006], pp. 61-62).

Question 4. By some counts Saul attempted to take David's life six times, some directly and others indirectly (for example, by making outrageous conditions for the marriage of his daughter that would usually result in his death). "It is a great thing to be a Jonathan. Without Jonathan, David was at risk of either abandoning his vocation and returning to the simple life of tending sheep or developing a murderous spirit of retaliation to get even with the man who was despising the best that was within him" (Peterson, *Leap Over a Wall*, pp. 54-55).

Questions 4-5. Peterson notes, "Jonathan's friendship entered David's soul in a way that Saul's hatred never did" (ibid., p. 53). Jonathan's relationship with David was complex, given the fact that Jonathan was the king's son and destined for the throne himself, though he affirmed that David should become king after Saul, at great cost to himself. So Jonathan is caught between his loyalty to and honoring of his father, as Scripture affirms (Exodus 20:12), and his love for and loyalty to David. How he navigates this triangle of love, jealousy and risk is a fascinating study in relational integrity.

Question 6. These friends call on God as "witness" (1 Samuel 20:12) of their sworn friendship. This recalls a much earlier "witness stone," Mizpah, between Jacob and his father-in-law Laban, as certifying that God would be watching over their relationship (Genesis 31:45-54). Earlier (1 Samuel 18:1) the text says that Jonathan "became one in spirit with David, and he loved him as himself." Jonathan gave him some of his personal and royal belongings as a symbol of their friendship. But later and only once are we told about David's feelings toward Jonathan, in the lament over his death: "your love to me was wonderful, passing the love of women. As a mother loves her only son, so I was loving you" (2 Samuel 1:26 Vulgate trans.). This has led some scholars to intimate that they had a homosexual relationship, though there is nothing in the story or text to indicate this.

The word *covenant* is used frequently in the narrative. A covenant is different from a contract. With a contract goods and services are exchanged with certain agreed-upon terms. If the terms are not met, the contract can be broken. A covenant is different. It is a relationship of belonging. Modeled after God's covenant with his people, a covenant is essentially relational. God says, as we say in marriage vows, "I am yours and you are mine." It is not a service contract by which God agrees to give us eternal salvation in exchange for sacrificial service in the church and world. Further, the covenant is essentially unconditional. That is, untoward circumstances should not break down the covenant. God agrees to be ours forever. Thence, in the marriage service a pastor often will say something like, "Such a covenant is not to be entered lightly or thoughtlessly but carefully and in reverence for God." Speaking to the uniqueness of covenant, Eric Rust says, "This was a form of relationship made in the presence of the Lord, in which each party accepted obligations toward the other; it was regarded as being of the same order as blood relationship. It was such that it could be described as the knitting together of the souls of the two men (18:1), by which was meant that the very being of the one extended into and embraced the personality of the other" (Rust, *Judges–Samuel*, p. 108). Biblical covenants involved two obligations: affection or love, and faithfulness. These two features were encompassed in the untranslatable Old Testament word *hesed*, which is usually rendered by phrases such as "lovingkindness" or "steadfast love," but it is not just love; it includes loyalty. For the application of this to marriage see R. Paul Stevens, *Married for Good: The Lost Art of Staying Happily Married* (Downers Grove, IL: InterVarsity Press, 1986). Such was the covenant of friendship between David and Jonathan.

Questions 7-8. Eugene Peterson makes an apt comment on how this story applies to ourselves. "Many a covenantal friendship is lived out in 'Saul's court'—in marital, family, work, and cultural conditions that are hostile to a vowed intimacy. But it's the covenant, not the conditions, that carries the day" (Peterson, *Leap Over a Wall*, pp. 53-54).

Question 9. It is significant in the continuing story of David as king that he continually turned to God for help in the most trying circumstances. The psalms of David are eloquent witness to this.

Question 11. Even after Jonathan had tragically died, David continued to be loyal to Jonathan after David became king by caring for Jonathan's son Mephibosheth (2 Samuel 9:1-3).

Study 7. Providing for One's Family. Proverbs 31:10-31.

Purpose: To discover how ordinary family life is practical ministry to those closest to us.

Questions 1-2. In this portion the woman's spiritual orientation is described as "fear of the Lord." "The fear of the Lord" (v. 30) is the starting point of Proverbs (1:7) and the beginning of true wisdom. Why? Because the character transformation that gaining wisdom involves, and practical know-how for life, are not mere human inventions. They come from a relationship with the living God, a relationship of affectionate reverence of God, being taught by God in life, as the servant in Isaiah says,

> The Sovereign LORD has given me an instructed tongue. . . .
> He wakens me morning by morning,
> wakens my ear to listen like one being taught.

Thus the servant knows "the word that sustains the weary" (Isaiah 50:4). Fear is not fright. But neither is it chumminess with God. Dr. Bruce Waltke shows that the fear of God has both emotional and rational components, like covenant love that has both affection and loyalty. (Bruce Waltke, "The Fear of the Lord: The Foundation for a Relationship with God" in *Alive to God: Studies in Spirituality*, ed. J. I. Packer and Loren Wilkinson [Downers Grove, IL: InterVarsity Press, 1992], pp. 17-33). The result in this woman is beautiful.

Here is a woman who is not silent, not sickly compliant to her husband, not frivolous, but truly beautiful inside, though we know nothing of her outside beauty. In comparison, external beauty and charm for a woman is "fleeting" (Proverbs 31:30). The question of how to gain the fruit of the Spirit (Galatians 5:22-23), so evident in this woman, is an important one. The critical question is how we receive that gift, and Galatians 5 gives us a real answer: by recognizing our neediness and bringing it to God, something Galatians describes as crucifying the sinful nature (v. 24) and walking with and imbibing the Spirit (v. 25).

Question 3. Through combining innovation with implementation new things can be created, new wealth created and new growth facilitated in a family or enterprise. Many inventions fail for lack of implementation, and some people languish in wishful dreaming, like the sluggard in the earlier Proverbs. But entrepreneurs are critical for the thriving of families and organizations. But who are entrepreneurs, and is this something we are born to or something we can learn? Most scholars on the subject recognize that while certain personality characteristics incline one to be an entrepreneur, it is something that can be learned, indeed called forth by a situation, a situation such as the day-to-day needs of a family. In study 5 we learned that we have a creative God who made creating creatures. So it is part of our God-imaging dignity that we can envision new things and implement possibilities. It is also positively inspired by the God who encourages risk and stewardship, as is so amply explained in the parable of the talents (Matthew 25:14-30), where the one-talent person shrunk from investment for fear of the master (vv. 24-25). Max Weber in his famous *The Protestant Ethic and the Spirit of Capitalism* argued that what inspires entrepreneurship is anxiety in persons unsure whether they were among those elected to eternal salvation in the context of later Calvinism. In reality Weber was examining post-Protestantism as the motivation for zealous work in the marketplace and thriftiness in saving and reinvestment. The fundamental motivation in people who know they have been saved by Christ and justified not by their works but through faith is gratitude. (See "The Spiritual and Religious Sources of Entrepreneurship: From Max Weber to the New Business Spirituality," *Crux* 36, no. 2 [2000]: pp. 22-33. See also Richard Goosen and R. Paul Stevens, *Entrepreneurial Leadership: Finding Your Calling, Making a Difference* [Downers Grove, IL: InterVarsity Press, 2013]. This connection between the triune God and co-creativity with God is explored in the classic book by Brian Griffiths, *The Creation of Wealth* [Downers Grove, IL: InterVarsity Press, 1985]; and a more recent book by Peter Bernstein, *Against the Gods: The Remarkable Story of Risk* [Hoboken, NJ: John Wiley & Sons, 1996]).

Questions 4-5. As outlined in the introduction most people associate "ministry" with a place (the church), special people (ministers) or sacred actions (administering the sacraments or preaching). Dualism, so epidemic in the worldwide church, gives the priority to sacred places, sacred actions and sacred moments, ignoring the presence of God and the potential for God-inspired service in everyday life. This pernicious dualism has been destroyed by the life, death and resurrection of Jesus, making everyday life—the necessary, the menial and the mundane—shot through with holiness and God-presence (see R. Paul Stevens, *Down-to-Earth Spirituality: Encountering God in the Ordinary, Boring Stuff of Life* [Downers Grove, IL: InterVarsity Press, 2003]).

Question 6. Workaholics typically keep long hours, talk a lot about their accomplishments, are unable to say no and cannot rest or relax. In many ways they appear to be similar to people zealously pursing a calling. The apostle Paul, for example, worked hard before and after he met Jesus, but the "after" came not from a feverish desire to win acceptance with God but sheer gratitude. Workaholics are self-oriented, trying to meet a deep personal need by their continuous and strenuous work (See "Drivenness," in *The Complete Book of Everyday Christianity*, ed. Robert Banks and R. Paul Stevens [Downers Grove, IL: InterVarsity Press, 1997], pp. 312-18). This woman is *other-oriented*, and her industriousness is not merely to meet some unmet need for acceptance or approval, but motivated by her neighborliness, her obedience to the second great commandment—loving the neighbor. This second commandment is motivated by the first commandment, to love of God wholeheartedly. Unlike so many so-called believers in the world today, she gets into her work heart and soul, as Paul admonished the Colossian slaves (Colossians 3:23). (This and some other comments in the notes are also found in R. Paul Stevens, *Work Matters: Lessons from Scripture* [Grand Rapids: Eerdmans, 2012], pp. 97-101.)

Tremper Longman translates Proverbs 31:13 this way: "She works with her hands *with pleasure*" (Tremper Longman III, *Proverbs* [Grand Rapids: Baker, 2006], p. 543). There are multiple joys in work. There is the joy of simply being able to work, the joy of using gifts and talents, the joy of knowing that others will benefit from our work. But the ultimate joy in work, here only in hint form (v. 30) is to enter into the joy of the Lord, which in the parable of Jesus is the ultimate spirituality of work: "Come and share your master's happiness" (Matthew 25:23). As a sign of this pleasure this woman makes fine clothing for herself—Egyptian linen and purple (Proverbs 31:22), both materials being suggestive of royalty. She makes covering for "her bed" (v. 22). And, as Longman notes, the reference to beautiful bed covering may have sensual overtones, as it certainly does in Proverbs 7:16, but if it does it is certainly understated (ibid., p. 545).

Questions 7-9. A previous generation thought that praising other members of the family "will make them proud." Ironically, becoming proud is the effect of not being praised. Children are pushed to succeed in academics or have spotless behavior to gain the approval of parents. The same happens in many marriages. People differ in respect to their needs. It is widely recognized that under the surface most people have a craving for one of these three: status, intimacy or power. Some personalities are what psychologists call "market oriented"; they will do almost anything to gain respect and approval. The servant songs in Isaiah 42:1-9, 49:1-7, 50:4-9, 52:13–53:12 reveal the true minister/servant of God as a person who finds approval in the pleasure of God and knowing that he or she is called of God. It is essential to find our identity in relation to God rather than the task. Consequently the servant—sometimes called "the servant of the Lord" and sometimes, "my servant" (when God is speaking), has profound respect for personality, especially people that are like broken reeds ready to snap, or smoldering wicks down to their last flicker (Isaiah 42:3). And the servant cares about the public arena and wants to bring justice (Isaiah 42:4).

Study 8. Building Unity. Romans 15:23-33; 1 Corinthians 16:1-4; 2 Corinthians 8:10-15.

Purpose: To see how the use of money can be a ministry.

Question 1. Paul has modestly described his missionary work to this point in Romans 15:19, which involved planting churches in most of the eastern Mediterranean. This is all the more remarkable in that Paul was normally mixing his evangelistic ministry with making tents for a living. We find his comment "there is no more place for me to work" strange. John Stott reflects, "His strategy was to evangelize the populous and influential cities, and plant churches there, and then leave to others the radiation of the gospel into the surrounding villages" (John R. W. Stott, *Romans: God's Good News for the*

World [Downers Grove, IL: InterVarsity Press, 1994], p. 382). The church in Rome was not established by Paul and so he has hesitated until now to visit there. Of the many reasons Paul has for visiting Rome, one is to regard Rome as a steppingstone to Spain, noted in verses 24, 28. Paul uses a special word for his desire to be "assisted," which probably means travel funds to facilitate his trip to Spain. "It undoubtedly meant more than good wishes and a valedictory prayer" (ibid., p. 385).

Question 2. It is not entirely certain why the Christians in Judea were poor. Some Jewish people in Jerusalem and Judea had, when they became Christians, lost their jobs, were excommunicated from the synagogue and were destitute. Famines had come and gone. The early sharing of everything in common in the first few months of the church (Acts 2:42-47; 4:32-37) was followed by the judicious distribution of funds for the care of widows in Jerusalem (Acts 6:1-7), later by a short-term famine relief project (Acts 11:27-30) and now, in Paul's mature ministry, with a long-term project to contribute materially to the needs of Jewish Christians back in Judea.

Commenting on the gift, Stott notes,

> The significance of the offering (the solidarity of God's people in Christ) was primarily neither geographical (from Greece to Judea), nor social (from the rich to the poor), nor even ethnic (from Gentiles to Jews), but both religious (from liberated radicals to traditional conservatives, that is, from the strong to the weak), and especially theological (from beneficiaries to benefactors). In other words, the so-called "gift" was in reality a "debt" (ibid., p. 386).

The Jews had contributed the law, prophets and, from their race, the Christ, and the Gentiles' churches were in debt to them. Paul uses the word *koinonia*, which means "common sharing" such as obtained in a business partnership, to describe the contribution to the saints. Paul asks the Romans to pray that the gift will be received. He realizes that the difficulty might be not merely receiving a gift that seems to put the recipient into debt with another but "in accepting the gift from Paul, Jewish Christian leaders would seem to endorse Paul's gospel and his seeming disregard of Jewish law and traditions. Yet if his offering were to be rejected, this could cause the rift between Jewish and Gentile Christians to widen irrevocably" (ibid., p. 389).

Question 4. Probably Paul has several things in mind in writing this letter. But one thing we know: in writing this letter he has explained "the gospel of God," especially as it relates to Jews and Gentiles together. The full blessing of Christ is the inworking and outworking of this glorious gospel of justification: it is the inscape and outscape of a person undergoing transformation (2 Corinthians 3:18; Romans 6:4). But more particularly it is the blessing of being included in Christ with people with whom one would otherwise have nothing to do. The Bible knows nothing of solitary religion, nothing of denominational isolationism, nothing of monocultural Christianity, nothing of mashed potato unity. (For a sermon on the significance of the three churches mentioned—Jerusalem, Rome and Spain—see R. Paul Stevens, "The Full Blessing of Christ," in *Romans and the People of God: Essays in Honor of Gordon D. Fee*, ed. Sven Soderlund and N. T. Wright [Grand Rapids: Eerdmans, 1999], pp. 295-303.) Paul notes the same theme in Ephesians 3:18 where it is only "together with all the Lord's people" that we can know how wide, long, high and deep the love of Christ is.

Question 5. By starting the chapter with "Now about the collection" Paul is almost certainly responding to something the Corinthians asked about the collection. For Paul the collection was not merely getting together a sum of money. In his letters he uses many different words—*fellowship, service, grace, blessing* and *divine service* (2 Corinthians 8:4, 6, 7; 9:1, 5, 12, 13; Romans 15:31) indicating that this offering "was for Paul an active response to the grace of God that not only ministered to the needs of God's people but also became a kind of ministry to God himself, which resulted in thanksgiving toward God and in a bond of fellowship between 'God's people' across the empire" (Gordon D. Fee, *The First Epistle to the Corinthians*. New International Commentary on the New Testament [Grand Rapids: Eerdmans 1987], p. 812). Significantly in verse 2 "there is no hint of a tithe or proportionate giving; the gift is simply to be related to their ability from week to week as they have been prospered by God" (ibid., p. 814).

Some may note that one remarkable omission in the New Testament are constant appeals to raise money for the support of Christian workers and for the provision of meeting places. The size of early churches has something to do with the latter omission as people met in homes and eventually took over Roman basilicas. But on the former, as we noted in study 3, most church leaders were tentmakers. Paul strongly affirmed the right of Christian leaders to be supported but refused that right for himself, for reasons noted earlier. Some challenging issues about the stewardship of personal and local church resources include relinquishing ownership to God, practicing thanksgiving and living with contentment, paying our taxes with a generous heart, giving directly to the poor with no strings attached, giving to God's global work (as the Romans would share in Paul's journey to Spain), and being ready, if so commanded, to sell all and follow Jesus.

Question 6. According to 2 Corinthians 8:10-11, the Corinthians had made a beginning but had failed to follow through with their gifts. So Paul sent Titus twice to bring the gift to completion. Paul had made a "painful visit" to Corinth, and their giving had lapsed. But eventually Paul's relationship with the Corinthians improved and, as we learn from Romans 15, the Corinthians made good on their original intention and even were "eager to do so."

Question 7. See the notes on question 5.

Study 9. Seeking the Welfare of the City. Jeremiah 29:1-23; Romans 16:23; Acts 19:21-22; 1 Peter 2:11-12.

Purpose: To learn how to combine service to the church and society at the same time.

Question 1. The background to this study may be important. A thumbnail sketch of Israel's history includes the family of Abraham, Isaac and Jacob going down to Egypt when Joseph was second in command; being delivered from eventual slavery there by Moses; wandering in the wilderness for forty years; entering the Promised Land under Joshua and becoming a tribal confederacy under God as their ruler. Then the people demanded a king, first Saul, then David and Solomon. On the death of Solomon the nation divided into two, the north now being called Israel and the south named after its major tribe, Judah. Meanwhile the superpower Assyria conquers the northern kingdom and takes thousands into captivity to their capital Nineveh. But the Assyrian power crumbled and Babylon emerged supreme and became God's instrument of judgment on a debased people of God by taking the southern kingdom into captivity in 587 B.C. Jeremiah the prophet was offered a comfortable life at court but chose to remain in Judah. But when the Babylon-appointed governor was assassinated, the people fled to Egypt taking Jeremiah with them. But before going he wrote to the exiles the letter we are studying.

Question 3. Many people in the group will lament that it is very hard to be righteous in a secularized, idolatrous and postmodern situation. But the situation in Babylon might have been worse! There would be little to support faith in a single God and the righteous life that is related to that.

Question 4. The familiar verse of Jeremiah 29:11 is usually read individually, that God has a good plan for each one of us. This of course is true. Many, however, have understood the plan to be a life blueprint to be followed exactly, and failing to do so leads to "doing God's second best." A better way of understanding this would be to consider the plan to be a purpose, a generalized determination of God to bless us and through us to bless others. This purpose can be woven into all the decisions we make leading us into the life and service of the kingdom of God. Many people suffer from what they regard as a bad decision somewhere along the way and feel they are no longer "in the plan." God redeems even our mistakes. The text is really a word to the people as a whole. And it is liberating to realize that Jesus as the head of the church has a good purpose in mind for us corporately.

Question 5. Many people shrink from speaking about "false teachers" and would prefer "alternative viewpoints." But the reality is that many people are offering dangerous, God-denying and Scripture-twisting teaching that has the effect of leading people away from single-minded love, obedience and service of God.

Question 6. The background to the role of Erastus may be important. In the Roman Empire citizens of some means were able to offer themselves as a benefaction to the city for a year of service or to establish some material gift to improve the city. It appears that Erastus served at his own expense as "the city's director of public works" (Romans 16:23). Bruce Winter explains,

> He was engaging in the time-consuming office of *aedile* [an honorary public office] during the year in which Romans was written. . . .[He] served the city at his own expense in an annually-elected public office. He provided, in addition, a benefaction which was judged to be appropriate to the importance of that office by the majority of the electors, *viz.* a year of service in the actual running of an important aspect of the city of Corinth. (Winter, *Seek the Welfare of the City*, pp. 195-96)

All the while Erastus was active in the church. Winter comments, "If this is correct, then there was no dichotomy in the thinking of the early church between the gospel/church ministry and the seeking the welfare of the city of Corinth as benefactors. . . . Paul wrote in such a way as to imply that the secular and spiritual welfare of the city were two sides of a single coin and not separate spheres" (ibid., pp. 196-97).

The church is actually a rhythm of gathering (for edification) and dispersion (for service and mission), much as the blood in the human body is gathered for cleansing and oxygenation and dispersed to bring nutrients, hormones and enzymes to every part of the body. So in one sense all the members are "sent" into the world in their homes, workplaces and civic responsibilities. In this case it may not have been Erastus's remunerated work that located him in city hall but a voluntary gift of himself. Behind this is something important in the Roman culture, that is, patrons and clients. The patrons looked after the clients, providing for them in return for the loyalty and service the client rendered to the patron. But one spectacular difference the influence of Christ made to Christians is that even the clients, those more dependent financially, were to become benefactors.

Question 7. While it is good for the church to send missionaries to other countries and cultures, it is a truism not actually realized that all the members are sent into workplaces, homes, government offices, hospitals and medical clinics, and social agencies. The Latin word for "send" is *missio*, from which we get the English word *mission*.

Questions 8-9. Winter comments, "The Christian social ethic . . . can only be described as an unprecedented social revolution of the ancient benefaction tradition. All able-bodied members of the Christian community were to seek the welfare of others in their city, even though they might be treated as 'foreigners'" (ibid., p. 209).

Study 10. Doing Something Beautiful for God. Mark 14:1-9.
Purpose: To discover how to do beautiful things for God.

Question 1. John's account of the same event includes Mary anointing Jesus' feet (John 12:3), wiping his feet with her hair, the fragrance filling the room. Washing and anointing feet for a visitor was the normal courtesy, but Mary goes "all out" and anoints both feet and head, and wipes the excess on the feet with her hair. Anointing at feasts was a common custom (Psalm 23:5; 141:5; Luke 7:46). Nard is an aromatic oil extracted from a root in India (William L. Lane, *Commentary on the Gospel of Mark*, New International Commentary on the New Testament [Grand Rapids: Eerdmans, 1974], p. 492).

The perfume, pure nard (John 12:2-3), was an imported fragrance from India kept in a sealed alabaster flask, both of great value. It may have been a family heirloom passed down from generation to generation. In order for the fragrance to be released, the neck of the flask had to be broken and a drop of the perfume, all that was needed for a customary anointing, poured out. Mary dispensed the entire contents on the head and feet of Jesus. The value of the vial and contents was roughly equivalent to a year's salary of a laborer.

Question 2. Paul Barnett notes that "The sensitivity and loyalty of this woman of Bethany is very different from the uncomprehending hostility of the male disciples, who at this point stand symbolically with the conspirators. They are indistinguishable from Jesus' opponents and outsiders" (Paul Barnett, *The Servant King: Reading Mark Today* [Sydney: Aquila Press, 1991], p. 261).

Question 4. The tradition of giving gifts to the poor during the Passover feast is well documented in the Jewish Talmud and Mishnah (biblical commentaries of the day). The celebrants were to give as charity one part of the second tithe normally spent in Jerusalem during the feast (Lane, *Commentary on the Gospel of Mark*, p. 493). Deuteronomy explains how people coming from a distance for the Jerusalem feast were to convert their tithe of animals and fruit to money and spend it in Jerusalem on good food and wine, "anything you wish" and, in effect, have a party (Deuteronomy 14:22-27). The original legislation involved remembering the Levites who were dependent on the gifts of others. In later times this became remembering the poor. Psalm 41 describes the blessing of "those who have regard for the weak" (41:1) and remarkably includes betrayal by a close friend (41:9). It is suggested that this psalm which speaks of the poor but righteous sufferer ultimately triumphing over his enemies may have been in her mind or that of Jesus. "The woman, unlike the dinner guests, perceived that Jesus is the poor man par excellence and her deed may be construed as an act of lovingkindness towards the poor" (ibid., pp. 493-94).

Question 5. The difference noted by Jesus is not between caring for the poor versus caring for Jesus, but between "always" having the poor and "not always" having him in the way that could be ministered to physically. Mary's work is better than almsgiving at this time, because it is more timely. Mary thought it not too much and neither did Jesus.

William Barclay notes that the exact word used by Jesus to describe Mary's act does not mean just morally good but something beautiful. "A thing might be *agathos* [morally good], and yet be hard, stern, austere, unattractive. But a thing which is *kalos* [beautiful] is winsome and lovely. . . . Love does not only do good things. Love does lovely things" (William Barclay, *The Gospel of Mark* [Edinburgh: Saint Andrew Press, 1960], pp. 342-43). In a very old reflection, A. Moody Stuart sums up the issue: "Christ loved the poor, gave himself for the poor, preached the gospel to the poor, and made himself poor that he might make the poor rich. If we love Christ we shall be like him, and we shall do good to the poor; even because we have them always, we shall seek always to do them good" (A. Moody Stuart, *The Three Marys: Mary of Magdala, Mary of Bethany, Mary of Nazareth* [Edinburgh: Banner of Truth Trust, 1984], p. 199).

Questions 6-7. Lane notes, "This pronouncement indicates that Jesus anticipated that he would suffer a criminal's death, for only in that circumstance would there be no anointing of the body" (Lane, *Commentary on the Gospel of Mark*, p. 494). But in prophesying that Mary's deed would be told throughout the world, Jesus was indicating that the gospel would be preached beyond the grave and that there would be resurrection after the death.